THE BOOK OF AMOS: A COMMENTARY

THE BOOK OF AMOS
A COMMENTARY

ERLING HAMMERSHAIMB

Translated by
JOHN STURDY

SCHOCKEN BOOKS · NEW YORK

Published in U.S.A. 1970
by Schocken Books Inc.
67 Park Avenue, New York, N.Y. 10016

© in this translation
Basil Blackwell, 1970

*Library of Congress Catalog
Card No.* 70–124678

This is a translation from the third
edition of *Amos Fortolket*, published
in 1967 by Nyt Nordisk Forlag,
Copenhagen.

Printed in Great Britain

PREFACE

This commentary first appeared in Danish in 1946. Its aim was to give students beginning the study of theology an introduction to the prophetic literature of the Old Testament. It was for this reason that I chose Amos to write on, as the prophetic book most suitable for beginners to study. My purpose led me to put the main emphasis on practice in exegetical method, while I largely omitted references to the scholarly literature when talking about different possibilities of interpretation. I was also anxious to work with the Hebrew text as we know it in the textual tradition of the Massoretes, and to avoid as far as possible making alterations in it. In a number of particularly difficult cases I have preferred to admit to failure in our understanding of the text.

Because of my conviction of the reliability of the Massoretic text, I have refrained from any attempt to reconstruct the text with the help of the metre. In my view the rhythm in Hebrew poetry is much freer than is generally allowed, and constantly varies in accordance with the nature of the subject-matter. It is only in exceptional cases that I have made comments on the metre in the commentary, and I would refer those interested to the literature on Hebrew metre.

The English text is not a slavish rendering of the Danish text. I have made a number of corrections and additions to the book after working through the text again. Many of these have been made at the suggestion of the translator of the book, the Rev. John Sturdy, to whom I would like to express my warm thanks.

I am grateful to my Danish publishers Arnold Busck for consenting to the production of an English version of the book, and to my English publishers for undertaking the publication of my book in English. I would also like to thank Prof. G. W. Anderson, at whose suggestion the translation was undertaken.

E. HAMMERSHAIMB

CONTENTS

COMMENTARY

ABBREVIATIONS

ANEP   *The Ancient Near East in Pictures Relating to the Old Testament*, ed. J. B. Pritchard, Princeton 1954

ANET   *Ancient Near Eastern Texts Relating to the Old Testament*, ed. J. B. Pritchard, Princeton, ed. 2, 1955

AOB   *Altorientalische Bilder zum Alten Testament*, ed. H. Gressmann, Berlin and Leipzig 1927

AOT   *Altorientalische Texte zum Alten Testament*, ed. H. Gressmann, Berlin and Leipzig 1926

BDB   *A Hebrew and English Lexicon of the Old Testament*, ed. F. Brown, S. R. Driver and C. A. Briggs, Oxford 1906

BH   *Biblia Hebraica*, edn. 3, ed. R. Kittel (minor prophets ed. O. Procksch), Stuttgart 1937

BRL   *Biblisches Reallexicon*, ed. K. Galling (Handbuch zum Alten Testament, vol. 1), Tübingen 1937

BWANT   Beiträge zur Wissenschaft vom Alten und Neuen Testament

CTA   *Corpus des tablettes en cunéiformes alphabétiques découvertes à Ras Shamra—Ugarit de 1929 à 1939*, ed. A. Herdner, Institut Français d'Archéologie de Beyrouth (Bibliothèque archéologique et historique 39, Mission de Ras Shamra Tome X), Paris 1963

FRLANT   Forschungen zur Religion und Literatur des Alten und Neuen Testaments

Gr.   *Gesenius' Hebrew Grammar as edited and enlarged by the late E. Kautzsch*, ed. 2, rev. and tr. A. E. Cowley, Oxford 1910

IDB   *The Interpreter's Dictionary of the Bible*, ed. G. A. Buttrick, 4 vols., Nashville 1962

JNES   *Journal of Near Eastern Studies*

KAI   *Kanaanäische und Aramäische Inschriften*, ed. H. Donner and W. Röllig, 3 vols., Wiesbaden 1962 and 1964

KB   L. Köhler and W. Baumgartner, *Lexicon in Veteris Testamenti Libros*, Leiden 1953, ed. 2, 1958

LXX   The Septuagint

MT   The Massoretic Text

NSI   *A Textbook of North Semitic Inscriptions*, ed. G. A. Cooke, Oxford 1903

NTT	*Norsk Teologisk Tidskrift*
OTS	*Oudtestamentische Studien*
RoB	*Religion och Bibel*
RV	Revised Version
RSV	Revised Standard Version
SEÅ	*Svensk Exegetisk Årsbok*
SVT	Supplements to Vetus Testamentum
VT	*Vetus Testamentum*
ZAW	*Zeitschrift für die Alttestamentliche Wissenschaft*

References to the Old Testament are to the Hebrew Bible's chapter and verse scheme. Where this differs from the English numeration it is noted in the RSV.

Ugaritic references are given on the scheme employed in *CTA*, which includes the older system of reference in brackets.

INTRODUCTION

The name of the prophet to whom the third of the books of the twelve minor prophets is ascribed is written in Hebrew עָמוֹס (not to be confused with the name of Isaiah's father Amoz, אָמוֹץ), and is borne by him alone in the Old Testament. Apart from the heading it is found again later in the book (7.8, 10 ff.; 8.2), but nowhere else. So we know nothing about the prophet other than what can be gathered from the book itself. According to the heading he was a shepherd from Tekoa, which is now known as Khirbet Teku'a, a little town in Judah about twenty kilometres south of Jerusalem. According to 7.14 he also kept cattle (assuming that the text is correct) and was concerned in the cultivation of sycamores, presumably as a sideline. Tekoa lies in a desolate area, surrounded by hills to the north and south-west; to the east the land slopes down to the Dead Sea, a good thousand metres below. Sycamore trees cannot grow at Tekoa, but down by the Dead Sea with its milder climate Amos could have cultivated them. The question must be left unanswered whether he owned the herd of sheep that he kept, or worked for the king or a landowner, with the right to a certain share of the offspring (cf. Gen. 30.25 ff.). Nor can we say with certainty whether Tekoa was his birthplace, or if it was only later that he made his living there together with the other shepherds who were called 'the shepherds from Tekoa' (1.1).

In 7.14, where he talks about his profession, he insists that he is not a prophet nor a disciple of a prophet. By this he means that he is not a prophet by profession, does not belong to a band of prophets, and has not uttered his prophecies for financial gain like the professional prophets, but because Yahweh had called him and compelled him to prophesy (cf. 3.8). Although he was from Judah, he appeared in the Northern Kingdom, in particular in Bethel with its well-known sanctuary (3.14; 4.4; 5.6; 7.10 ff.), but had apparently also been in Samaria and spoken there (see 4.1 ff., cf. 3.9 ff. and 6.1 ff.). The book rather gives the impression that his prophetic activity only extended over a short period of time.

Before his appearance as a prophet Amos probably knew several of the towns of the Northern Kingdom from personal
experience. His occupation may have involved travelling around
with his flocks or going to the markets of the Northern Kingdom
to sell his products there. His speeches in any case witness to a
thorough knowledge of the situation there. He has been present
at the great pilgrimage festivals, where the participants come
streaming in to the great sanctuaries, he knows how rich men and
their wives live in luxury and carouse in magnificent palaces, he is
familiar with the corruption of the judges and their partiality
against the poor, and he has seen with indignation the confident
expectation of the people that the day of Yahweh will bring them
good fortune and success, in spite of their failure to fulfil Yahweh's moral demands. These experiences form the background
for his appearance as Yahweh's prophet in the Northern Kingdom. The impetus to leave his home and go to the North came,
so far as we can tell, through an inner revelation, in which he
heard Yahweh's command to go and proclaim judgement (3.8 and
7.15, cf. also the visions in chapters 7–9).

Amos not only knows the land of Israel, however; he is also
familiar with his people's history and the accounts of Yahweh's
acts of kindness to the people. For him Yahweh is the creator
God, who has led the people out of Egypt and preserved them
during the forty years of wandering in the wilderness, and then
defeated the Amorites in the land of Canaan, so that Israel could
dwell there (2.9 ff.; 9.7). He knows too that Yahweh has continuously cared for the spiritual well-being of the people, and
sent prophets to speak to the people and remind them of his
commandments (2.11). Amos does not therefore regard himself
as proclaiming something completely new, but feels himself akin
to the prophets whom Yahweh from time to time raised up among
the people to castigate and admonish them. He shows thereby
that he is in contact with circles which have preserved the tradi-
tions from the earliest days of the people. Consequently Amos
cannot have been a completely simple and uneducated shepherd.
His utterances show also that he was a master of the Hebrew
language. He displays an expert freedom in the use of different
verse forms one after another, and varies them with the content.
At times he breaks into prose or inserts brief comments which fall
outside the metre.

In Bethel he had a violent clash with the high-priest Amaziah as a consequence of his prophecies of disaster for the country, its sanctuary and the royal family. Amaziah regarded his proclamation of judgement as a danger to the security of the state, and reported the matter to king Jeroboam, with the result that Amos was expelled (7.10–17).

Amos' prophetic activity took place during the reign of Jeroboam II (c. 783–743), which roughly coincides with that of Uzziah in the Southern Kingdom (c. 775–735). The heading of the book fixes the time of Amos' first appearance as 'two years before the earthquake'. This is referred to also in Zech. 14.5, and must have been unusually violent, since it was used to date events by; but as we do not know anything more definite about it, this information is not of value to us. The book itself confirms that it comes from the time of Jeroboam II, after his victories in the lands east of the Jordan, where he had recovered part of the land which Israel had earlier been forced to abandon (6.13, cf. 2 Kgs. 14.25). In consequence the people were elated with victory, and confident that Yahweh was with them. Assyria, which was soon to make itself felt in Syria and Palestine with overwhelming force, is not yet seen as a power to fear. We can therefore fix the period of Amos' prophetic activity in the years about 750.

The book of Amos is divided into nine chapters. Chapters 1 and 2 consist of a series of threats, first directed to Israel's neighbours (Damascus, the Philistines, Tyre, Edom, Ammon and Moab), but ending with Judah and Israel. Chapters 3–6 are a collection of prophetic sayings primarily of a threatening nature; some are introduced with the set phrase, 'Hear this word!' (3.1; 4.1; 5.1), others with 'Woe!' (5.18; 6.1). Israel, because it is the chosen people, is to be punished more severely than other peoples for its sins. The rich are castigated for their self-indulgence and perversion of justice; the women for their luxury at the expense of the poor. Far from feeling pleasure in the sacrifices and feasts of the people, Yahweh actually hates them; he demands that the people should love the good and uphold justice. In contrast to the expectation of the people that the day of Yahweh will be light, Amos declares that it will be darkness, and that because of Israel's sins Yahweh will raise a people against them so that they will have to go into exile beyond Damascus. Chapters 7–9 are of strongly mixed content. A series of five visions concerning the ruin of

Israel (7.1–3; 4–6; 7–9; 8.1–3; 9.1–4) is broken off after the third vision for the clash with the high-priest Amaziah in Bethel, which has already been mentioned (7.10–17). After the fourth vision follows an oracle which is introduced by 'Hear!', and in content resembles the oracles of judgement in chapters 3 ff. The fifth vision is followed by a song of praise to Yahweh (9.5–6), after which comes another threat against Israel (9.7–10). The book concludes with a generous promise to the people of the restoration of the fallen booth of David and abundant fertility in the land (9.11–15).

From this description of the contents it can be seen that the book of Amos is not arranged on a consistent and systematic plan. This can best be seen in chapters 7–9, where it is clear that the oracle of 8.4 ff. which is introduced by 'Hear this!' is not in place; it belongs together with the other oracles in chapters 3 ff., which have a similar introductory formula. Similarly it is clear that the account of Amos' conflict at Bethel does not fit in with the visions, which are told in the first person. It really marks the end of his activity, and should therefore have been placed at the close of the book. The want of an ordered plan to the book suggests that it was not put together by Amos himself but by others, possibly by his own disciples. It is difficult to say with confidence what the principles are which are used in its arrangement. It has been suggested that there were in the first place smaller collections of oracles of judgement and visions (including the oracles against foreign nations in chapters 1 and 2, and the visions in chapters 7–9), and possibly a biography of Amos in prose. A fragment of this has then been inserted on the catchword principle after the third vision (cf. 7.9 with 7.10 ff.). Even if this theory of the composition of the book is basically correct it must be emphasized that by no means all the literary difficulties have found a satisfactory explanation through it, and that the catchword principle can only be applied successfully to a few passages. In hardly any cases can it be demonstrated convincingly how much of the book's present arrangement goes back to the prophet himself and how much to those who gave the book its final form.

This does not, however, affect the genuineness of the sayings. On the contrary, there is little against accepting that almost all the book goes back to Amos himself. This is true both of the poetic parts, which have very possibly preserved exactly the form in which they were delivered by Amos, and the prose account in 7.10–17, which may be based on his own report of the occasion. Indeed most of the book could have been written down in small sections by Amos himself (if he could write) or dictated by him to his disciples. The origin of the book can be ascribed to the wish of the prophet after his expulsion to show his fellow country-men and posterity that he had fulfilled his mission. When the punishment came men would be able to see that he had been right in his proclamation of judgement. There are many, however, who maintain that the speeches were first transmitted orally for a period, before they were written down and put in order, either by his disciples or by men living even later. In that case many other motives for the compilation of the book could have played a part, including the wish to collect all that could be found of the words of the prophet.

Doubts about authenticity have been raised especially over the threats against Tyre, Edom and Judah (1.9–10, 11–12; 2.4–5), the doxologies (4.13; 5.8–9; 9.5–6) and the concluding promise (9.11–15). The threats against Tyre and Edom, it has been argued, are constructed on a different pattern from the other threats, and the speech against Judah has been denied to Amos because his field of work was the Northern Kingdom, and because Deutero-nomistic influence is found in it. Lastly the concluding promises are taken to be secondary because they are felt to be inconsistent with Amos' preaching of the complete destruction of the people. In the commentary on the relevant passages these arguments are discussed, but it may be mentioned now that there are also weighty grounds for maintaining that Amos took a brighter view of the future of the people after the punishment.

The text is one of the best preserved among the prophetic books, and in only very few passages are there good reasons to assume a textual corruption.

COMMENTARY

CHAPTER ONE

V. 1. In an introductory heading we are given the name of the author of the book, his profession and home, and the time of his prophetic activity. From the perfect הָיָה in the words אֲשֶׁר הָיָה בַנֹּקְדִים 'who was one of the shepherds', it does not follow that at the time the heading was written he was no longer a shepherd but a prophet; he probably only gave up his original profession for a time, and went back to it after his expulsion from the Northern Kingdom (see on 7.10–17). But it can be concluded from the perfect הָיָה that the heading was written after the time of Amos by someone who wished to explain who this Amos was whose words follow. הָיָה בְּ, literally 'was among', means 'belonged to'. נֹקֵד is found in the Old Testament only here and in 2 Kgs. 3.4. In Arabic *naqad* is the name of a particular breed of sheep (they are proverbially ugly, but produce exceptionally good wool); the derivative noun *naqqād* signifies one who watches over this sort of sheep. The Hebrew participle is used in a corresponding manner. In 2 Kgs. 3.4 Mesha King of Moab is described as a נֹקֵד, who paid the king of Israel tribute of 100,000 lambs and the wool of 100,000 rams. The king must have had numerous shepherds under him to watch such huge flocks as are here spoken of. The king in Jerusalem may possibly have been the owner of large herds of sheep. From Ugarit the title *rb nqdm* 'head of the shepherds' is known (6 (I AB) VI, 55). Since it occurs in parallel to *rb khnm*, 'the high priest', it must be the title of an official of the temple. The origin of this is no doubt that the temples themselves owned flocks which were watched by shepherds under the direction of a special official. This allows the possibility that Amos was the shepherd of flocks of sheep that were owned by the temple in Jerusalem, so that in this way he had a certain

connection with the temple; but it can be no more than a possibility. He may of course have been employed by the king or by
a rich man as shepherd with a share in the offspring, or perhaps
himself have been the owner of the flocks.[1]

מִתְּקוֹעַ can be taken either with the immediately preceding word
בַּנֹּקְדִים or with עָמוֹס. In the former case the meaning does not
strictly have to be that Tekoa was his home; he could have been
admitted later to the ranks of the shepherds who worked in the
countryside around Tekoa. It is, however, most reasonable to
assume that the town was his birthplace. Tekoa is known to us as
the town from which Joab fetched the wise woman who persuaded David to bring Absalom back from exile (2 Sam. 14). The
second relative clause, introduced by אֲשֶׁר, should not be connected with the word Amos ('he who saw concerning Israel', too
indefinite a characterization of his prophetic activity), but with
דִּבְרֵי: 'the words which he saw concerning Israel'. The verb חָזָה
'see', 'behold' is used rather less frequently than רָאָה, the general
word for 'see', but can be used as a synonym for it in poetry (e.g.
Isa. 33.17). Both verbs are used of prophetic visions. From the
root חזה a number of nouns are derived which are connected
with the prophetic experience, among them חֹזֶה 'seer' and חָזוֹן
'vision'. Since one cannot 'see' words, the verb must be used
here in a more general sense of prophetic experiences, which included not only visions but also words, most frequently serving
as explanations of the visions (cf. chapters 7–9). It is expressed
more correctly in the heading of the book of Isaiah, 'the vision of
Isaiah, which he saw' (Isa. 1.1), or in the heading of the book of
Hosea, 'the word of Yahweh, which came to Hosea' (Hos. 1.1).
On the other hand in Isa. 2.1 a similar construction is found to the
one here. עַל 'concerning', often has a nuance of 'to the disadvantage of'. יִשְׂרָאֵל no doubt means here the Northern Kingdom, as
at the end of the verse. It is not, however, excluded that it could
mean all Israel, since at some places in the book, although ad-
mittedly only a few, references are found to Judah (2.4 f.; 6.1;
7.12; 9.11 f.). These are regarded by many commentators as later

---

[1] In Babylonia a distinction was made (in the Neo-Babylonian period) between *rabi-
bûli*, *nâqidu* and *rê'û*. In the first category are a small number of men who are responsible
for the temples' massive flocks, and under them numerous *nâqidu*, who again have the
actual shepherds, the *rê'û*, under them (see M. San Nicolò, 'Materialien zur Viehwirt-
schaft in den neubabylonischen Tempeln', *Orientalia* NS 17 (1948), pp. 284 f.).

insertions, but without adequate grounds. On Amos' use of
'Israel' see further on 2.6.

The rest of the verse contains two datings for Amos' activity.
The first dates his appearance to the days of Uzziah king of
Judah (c. 775–735) and of Jeroboam son of Joash king of Israel,
i.e. Jeroboam II (c. 783–743), as distinct from Jeroboam son of
Nebat, i.e. Jeroboam I. The name in Hebrew can be read either as
Yarob'am or as Yorob'am. The Babylonian Jews read it as יְרָבְעָם.
The form Jeroboam in the English versions is connected most
closely with the LXX's form Ἱεροβοαμ. The other dating fixes
the prophet's appearance as 'two years before the earthquake'.
Earthquakes are more frequent in Palestine than in northern Eur-
ope. The one that is referred to must have been specially violent,
since events could be dated by it (cf. Introduction, p. 13). Among
the catastrophes that Amos had predicted Yahweh would punish
his people with were earthquakes (see 8.8 and 9.1 ff.). Since a
violent earthquake in fact occurred two years later, his prophecy
was remembered, and this was seen as a fulfilment of it, and used
to fix the time of his appearance. But it also follows that the heading is not an intrinsic part of the book. It must in any case have
been written after the earthquake, but near enough to it for men
to remember clearly both this and Amos' appearance. Perhaps the
heading was written in several stages. The last dating is then the
oldest. The description of his profession may also be a later expansion on the basis of 7.14, so that the verse originally ran: the
words of Amos from Tekoa, which he saw concerning Israel two
years before the earthquake.

V. 2 stands like a motto before the preaching of Amos: Yahweh is wroth, and reveals himself for judgement. ויאמר is linked
on to v. 1 to develop the content of his visions and words. In this
way a transition is obtained from the heading to the book itself.
By immediately mentioning Yahweh's name Amos shows that
the cause of his appearance is Yahweh's revelation to him.
Although Yahweh has his dwelling-place in heaven (see 9.6),
Amos can also say that he dwells in Zion. It was here that the ark
was brought by David, and under Solomon found its final place
in the temple on the occasion of its consecration. No Judean
thereafter doubted that Yahweh had his home on Zion. It comes
naturally to Amos therefore to say that Yahweh utters his voice
from Zion, but this does not prevent his being able to appear in

other places. He can appear where he wishes on the whole earth, indeed in the whole universe (see 9.1 ff.[1]).

צִיּוֹן is originally the name of the citadel of the Jebusites which lay on the south-eastern hill of Jerusalem. After David's capture of it the name was taken over for his citadel, 'the city of David'. Later it became the name for the hill to the east, including the temple, and finally it was used for the whole city of Jerusalem, so that it can, as here, be used in parallelism with Jerusalem.

It is not clear where the images in the verse are derived from. Some have pointed out that 'the voice of Yahweh' is a general expression for thunder (Ps. 18.14; 29.3 ff.; Exod. 19.16, etc.). But since thunder is normally accompanied by rain, it does not fit well here, where the result is a withering of all vegetation (v. 2b). Others have therefore thought of a different kind of storm, e.g. a loud earthquake accompanied by a devastating desert wind. For this cf. Joel 4.16, the first half-verse of which is identical with v. 2a, but of which the continuation, 'and the heavens and the earth shake', is easier to understand than 2b. Others again maintain that Yahweh is compared to a lion which roars when it goes hunting before rushing at its prey (cf. the verb שָׁאַג in 3.4 and 8). As the lion's roar portends devastation and death, Yahweh's voice is a sign of his wrath, which will result in devastation in the natural world (cf. Jer. 2.15). The second half-verse in any case describes a drought so extensive that it affects both the pastures, which Amos as a shepherd thinks of first and foremost, and the forest on the top of Carmel, which every Israelite knew at least by name (1 Kgs. 18). The expressions chosen do in fact imply the devastation of the whole land.

אבל 'mourn' (for the dead). The rites of mourning include disfiguring oneself, putting on mourning clothes and scattering dust on one's head. When nature, which also is a living thing, mourns, this can be seen by the vegetation withering, and everything becoming waste (Isa. 24.4; 33.9). 'Mourn' is therefore a synonym for 'wither', cf. the parallel יָבֵשׁ (see also Jer. 12.4; 23.10).[2] נְאוֹת 'pastures'; the singular is נָוֶה (ו and א can be interchanged between two vowels in Semitic) from the root נוה, which in Arabic is

---

[1] On the origin, different forms and meaning of the name Yahweh see KB s.v., and H. Ringgren, *Israelite Religion*, London 1966, pp. 32 f.

[2] For the semantic connection of 'wither' with 'mourn' cf. also Assyrian *abālu* 'to be dry'.

known in the sense of 'to seek an objective', especially of nomads
who are looking for pasture. הַכַּרְמֶל is the well-known promontory which juts out into the Mediterranean west of Lake Gennesaret. The word is used with the article, because in origin it is a
common noun ('orchard'), which has come to be used as a name
(Gr. § 125e). The mountain is thickly covered with luxuriant
vegetation, including large trees. Carmel is also the name of a
hill-country village west of the Dead Sea (Josh. 15.55; 1 Sam.
25.2ff.), but this does not come into consideration here, since there
is a mention of the top of Carmel.

The uncertainty of the connection between the two half-verses
and the identity of the first half-verse with Joel 4.16a (cf. also
Jer. 25.30) have caused many commentators to deny the verse to
Amos. It is, however, by no means certain that the verse in Amos
is inserted from Joel, since this book has many other verses which
are dependent on other prophets. The connection between the
two half-verses does not become any easier if it is assumed that
the whole verse is a later insertion, of which half is taken from
Joel 4.16. In any case it should be clear that as the verse now reads
it is placed here as a summary of Amos' preaching and an introduction to the threats which follow.

1.3–2.16: *a series of oracles of judgement against the neighbours of
Israel.* Yahweh's wrath does not affect nature, as in v. 2, but men.
First Yahweh speaks against the surrounding peoples: the Aramaeans, the Philistines, the Phoenicians, the Edomites, the Ammonites and the Moabites. Then he turns against Judah and
finally against the Northern Kingdom. The individual threats are
all constructed on approximately the same pattern. First it is
stated in a standard formula that sin has been committed to ex-
cess. Then follows a declaration of what the sin consists in, and
finally a declaration of the punishment. Each of the oracles against
the different peoples forms a rounded unit in itself, but they were
no doubt put together (by Amos himself) with an eye to rhetorical
effect.[1] The prophet captures the attention of the Israelites by
uttering threats against the enemies of the land. This was also

---

[1] According to A. Bentzen, Amos makes use of a ritual pattern which has a parallel in
the Egyptian execration texts ('The Ritual Background of Amos 1.2–2.16', *OTS* 8
(1950), pp. 85–99).

done by the prophets of success, but Amos all the time gives reasons for the punishments in terms of breaches of a universally valid moral law; and as the prophet gradually comes nearer to Israel itself he hints that they too because of their transgressions will not escape scot-free. The threat against Israel is expressed more explicitly than the others, because the prophet has reached his proper subject. Collections of sayings against foreign nations similar to Amos 1.3–2.3 are found in Isa. 13–23, Jer. 46–51 and Ezek. 25–32, but there is a not insignificant difference that Amos has put together these oracles to show that no people which has sinned escapes punishment, while for the other prophets the concern is on the contrary to describe the well-earned judgement which befalls the enemies of Israel, to the delight of the listeners or readers of these prophets.

Vv. 3–5: The threat against Syria

V.3. The introduction is made, as in each of the following oracles, by use of the words: 'Thus has Yahweh said'. By this the prophet emphasizes that his utterance has divine authority, and four of the sayings underline this further by ending with: 'says (the Lord) Yahweh' (v. 5; 8; 15; 2.3). The expression 'for three transgressions, yes, for four I will not take it back' is repeated to introduce all the threats in 1.3–2.16. The variation between the number three in the first half of the verse and four in the second half is an example of a common use of parallelism as a stylistic variation, in which a number is given and then followed by the next higher number. There are examples for one and two (Ps. 62.12; Job 33.14), two and three (Hos. 6.2), six and seven (Job 5.19), and seven and eight (Mic. 5.4; Eccles. 11.2). This form of parallelism is very old, and occurs already in the Amarna letters and in the Ras Shamra texts (4 (II AB) III, 17 f.: 'two sacrifices does Baal hate, three the rider on the heavens'). The point behind the mention of three and four is that one sin of this sort would have been serious enough, but they have committed three or four of them. The basic meaning of פָּשַׁע is 'to rebel', 'to fall away', originally of rebellion against an earthly overlord (1 Kgs. 12.19; 2 Kgs. 1.1), then of rebellion against God, i.e. sin (Isa. 1.2; Jer. 2.8). The corresponding noun פֶּשַׁע is similarly used both of offences against other men, and of offences against God. Here it is used for the misdeeds the Aramaeans committed against the population of Gilead. Damascus is emphasized as being the most important city in Syria, and the capital of the largest of the Aramaean kingdoms.

The city lies in a fertile valley with plentiful supplies of water from the two rivers Abana and Pharpar (2 Kgs. 5.12), which rise on Hermon and the Antilibanus respectively, about forty kilometres to the west and north-west. The city has since very early days been on the caravan route from Mesopotamia to Palestine and further to the south along the Mediterranean to Egypt, or through Transjordan to the Gulf of Akaba and to Arabia (see *BRL*, cols. 260–5). It therefore occupied an important commercial and strategic position from an early time. Its non-semitic name, which already occurs in the Amarna letters, could suggest that it was not founded by Semites. About 1200 B.C. the Aramaeans seized power in the city after the fall of the Hittite kingdom. From the time of David we have the first reports of conflicts with Israel. The Aramaeans of Damascus had supported the Aramaean king Hadad'ezer of Ṣoba against David, who, however, conquered the Aramaeans, put garrisons into Aram of Damascus, and made it tributary (2 Sam. 8.3 ff.). In Solomon's time the suzerainty was lost, when Rezon, one of the subjects of Hadad'ezer of Ṣoba, fled from his master, and made himself leader of a marauding band. He captured Damascus and became king there (1 Kgs. 11.23–5). Benhadad I was at first in treaty relationship with king Baasha of Israel, but was bribed by king Asa of Judah to break with him, and ravaged and captured a part of the country (1 Kgs. 15.18–20). His son Benhadad II suffered defeat twice at the hands of Ahab (1 Kgs. 20.1–34); in a later battle for Ramoth-Gilead Ahab, who had obtained the support of king Jehoshaphat of Judah, was killed (1 Kgs. 22.1–38). Benhadad II was slain by Hazael, who became king in place of him (2 Kgs. 8.7–15). He fought another battle at Ramoth-Gilead, but this time the opponents of the Aramaeans were Ahab's son Joram and Ahaziah of Judah (2 Kgs. 8.28 f.). During the reign of Jehu Hazael inflicted a severe defeat on Israel. In his perilous position Jehu called on Shalmaneser III king of Assyria for help, and paid tribute to him in 841. Shalmaneser undertook a campaign against Damascus, but could not conquer the city, and had to confine himself to cutting down the orchards around it (see *AOT*, p. 343, *ANET*, p. 280). When this campaign was over, Hazael

continued the fight against Israel, and conquered large parts of Transjordan (2 Kgs. 10.32 f.). He even marched into the land west of the
Jordan, where he captured the Philistine city of Gath, and threatened to march against Jerusalem; king Joash of Judah was, however,
successful in buying him off (2 Kgs. 12.18 f.). The strong pressure
against Israel was continued by Hazael and by his son Benhadad III
in the reign of Jehu's son Jehoahaz, and Israel's forces were reduced
to a minimum (2 Kgs. 13.3–7). There was a perceptible alleviation
when the Assyrians conquered Damascus in 805. After this Jehoahaz' son Joash was successful in defeating Benhadad III three
times and took from him the cities which he had conquered from his
father Jehoahaz (2 Kgs. 13.25). The advance continued under
Joash's son Jeroboam II, who not only reconquered all of the Israelite territory east of the Jordan down to the Dead Sea, but also
pressed on into Aramaean territory (Amos 6.13; 2 Kgs. 14.25;
according to v. 28 he even conquered Damascus and Hamath, but
only for a time).

Apart from the largest Aramaean kingdom, of which Damascus
was the capital, and the Aram Ṣoba already mentioned (2 Sam. 10.6,
8), there were various other small Aramaean kingdoms, which were
similarly named after their capitals, such as Aram Beth Reḥob
(2 Sam. 10.6), Aram Maacah (1 Chr. 19.6) and Aram Naharaim (Aram
of the two rivers, i.e. Mesopotamia, see Gen. 24.10). In Amos' time
it is possible that Damascus had suzerainty over the smaller Aramaean kingdoms, or it may be that he singles out Damascus in 1.3
as the most important city as he does Gaza among the Philistine
cities in the following section (see v. 6).

The Israelites regarded themselves as related to the Aramaeans,
in that both had Shem as their ancestor (Gen. 10.21 f.). The stories
about Jacob and Laban the Aramaean reflect both the kinship of the
two peoples and their constant struggles in older times (see Gen.
28–32). From the study of Assyrian and Babylonian cuneiform
texts our knowledge of the earliest history of the Aramaeans has
been significantly increased in recent years (see the article 'Aramu'
by E. Forrer in *Reallexicon der Assyriologie*, ed. E. Ebeling and B.
Meissner, Berlin and Leipzig, vol. 1, 1932, pp. 131–9, A. Dupont-
Sommer, *Les Araméens*, Paris 1949, W. F. Albright, 'Syria, the
Philistines, and Phoenicia', *Cambridge Ancient History*, vol. 2, new
ed., ch. 33, Cambridge 1966 (issued separately, fasc. 51). From about
the year 1100 the Aramaeans began to press into Assyria and Baby-

Ionia from the Syrian desert. They seem to have settled primarily as trading peoples and to have dominated trade in these kingdoms. Although they were completely absorbed by the local population their language came to be of enormous importance through being used as an international language not only in these kingdoms, but also later after the fall of Babylon in 539 in the Persian empire, where all royal edicts were promulgated in Aramaic, at least in the western part of the empire, including Egypt. From 2 Kgs. 18.26 (cf. Isa. 36.11) we learn that the leading officials in Jerusalem could speak Aramaic, and would be able to conduct a conversation with the Assyrian commanders in this language. After the exile Aramaic gradually replaced Hebrew as the vernacular. We cannot say for sure when this process was finally completed, but it had in any case happened by the time of Jesus. In the Old Testament there are some smaller sections written in Aramaic: Ezra 4.8–6.18; 7.12–26, and Daniel 2.4b–7.28 (besides the two words in Gen. 31.47 and the single verse Jer. 10.11). Closely related to Biblical Aramaic is the language of the Aramaic papyri from Elephantine, an island in the Nile (fifth century B.C.).[1] From a later period in the development of the language we have Jewish Aramaic (in the Targum, the Jerusalem Talmud and the Babylonian Talmud), Samaritan, Christian Palestinian Aramaic, Mandaic and Syriac (see further on this subject F. Rosenthal, *Die aramaistische Forschung seit Th. Nöldeke's Veröffentlichungen*, Leiden 1939 (reprinted 1964), and R. A. Bowman, 'Arameans, Aramaic, and the Bible', *JNES* 7 (1948), pp. 65–90).

The suffix in אֲשִׁיבֶנּוּ is in the neuter. It refers to the punishment which Yahweh will not now hold back any longer. The suffix could, however, refer to Assyria, which is to carry out the punishment (vv. 4–5 say what the punishment is). The offence of the Aramaeans consists in having 'threshed Gilead with threshing sledges of iron'. Threshing can be carried out by the primitive method of driving oxen over the corn on a threshing floor, until they have trodden out the grain with their hooves (Deut. 25.4; Mic. 4.13), or it can be done with the help of a threshing sledge

---

[1] See A. Cowley, *Aramaic Papyri of the Fifth Century B.C.*, Oxford 1923, and E. G. Kraeling, *The Brooklyn Museum Aramaic Papyri*, New Haven 1953. The Aramaic language in the period of the Persian empire is often called 'Reichsaramäisch' (imperial Aramaic) after J. Markwart and H. H. Schaeder, but is better called 'Standard Aramaic' (E. G. Kraeling).

(חָרוּץ, literally 'cutting', with the word מוֹרַג understood 'threshing sledge', cf. Isa. 41.15). This is a pair of roughly shaped
boards, bent upwards at the front and mounted with iron points
or with sharp stones (see I. Benzinger, *Hebräische Archäologie*,
ed. 3, Leipzig 1927, p. 145, *IDB* s.v. Threshing, vol. 4, p. 636).
The sledge is drawn by a pair of oxen over the corn until the
grain is separated from the husk. Finally according to Isa. 28.27
there seems to be also a threshing cart, but the text does not describe it in detail. Threshing with iron threshing sledges is certainly not to be understood literally here, with the Aramaeans
driving threshing sledges over their captives as a crude form of
torture, but to be taken figuratively of harsh treatment of those
they have conquered in general. The seriousness lies not so much
in the conquest of the land as in the inhuman treatment to which
the population has been subjected (cf. v. 13). The harsh treatment
is emphasized by the word 'iron'.[1] The infinitive דּוּשׁ is given a
pronominal suffix, which refers to the subject of the action, and is
also constructed with the object אֶת־הַגִּלְעָד (cf. Gr. § 58c). Gilead
is the name of the Israelite part of the land east of the Jordan. A
city of this name is mentioned a number of times in the Old
Testament (Judg. 10.17; 12.7; Hos. 6.8; 12.12). Here it refers to
the land, which had suffered during the constant fighting between
Syria and Israel, particularly in the time of Hazael, when the
Aramaeans pressed very hard upon the Israelites (cf. above).

V.4. As a consequence of (cf. the perfect consecutive) these
offences Yahweh will cause the royal palaces to be burnt down.
The fire means the fire of war, since towns were often burnt down
after they had been taken, or during the capture itself while fighting was going on from house to house. The same expression is
found again in vv. 7, 10, 12; 2.2 and 5. In 1.14 the verb 'kindle'
is used instead of 'send'. For the expressions cf. also Hos. 8.14;
Jer. 17.27. 'The house of Hazael', as the parallel expression 'the
palaces of Benhadad' shows, does not mean the royal house or
dynasty, but the royal citadel which Hazael had built, or simply
the citadel where he dwelt. Benhadad is perhaps Hazael's son,

---

[1] Iron בַּרְזֶל had been introduced long before the time of Amos. The Iron Age begins
in Palestine about 1200 B.C., in Syria somewhat earlier; for instance an iron axe has been
found at Ras Shamra from about 1400 B.C., and the expression *kkrm brẓl* 'two talents of
iron' occurs in accounts (C. Virolleaud, 'Lettres et Documents Administratifs Provenant
des Archives d'Ugarit', *Syria* 21 (1940), p. 274, *CTA* 141, l. 6). The word בַּרְזֶל points
to a non-semitic origin.

Benhadad III (see above), but could also be one of the older
kings of this name, from whom the palace took its name. אַרְמְנוֹת
(found twelve times in Amos) means the expensive houses which
kings and rich men built for their dwelling places in the large
cities. According to KB the word means 'dwelling-tower', i.e. a
fortified house with a small ground-floor area and with several
storeys. In contrast to the houses of the poor, which were built
of wood, or were mud-and-wattle huts, these were built of
dressed stone and had panels on the walls for decoration, and
luxurious furniture.

V. 5. As part of the defence of cities the city gate was equipped
with solid bars (בריח) of iron or bronze (1 Kgs. 4.13). When these
had been broken the entrance to the city was open to the besiegers
(cf. Jer. 51.30; Lam. 2.9). Damascus is mentioned first as the
most important city in Syria. In the next half-verse יוֹשֵׁב could be
a collective for 'the inhabitants', but is better taken as 'the ruler'
(literally 'he who sits', i.e. on the throne, see Isa. 10.13, and
cf. Ps. 2.4; 22.4), parallel with the following 'him that holds
the sceptre', an old description for the ruler (cf. the expression
אחז חטר in the Aramaic Hadad inscription from Zenjirli (first half of
the eighth century B.C.), lines 15, 20, 25, see *NSI*, pp. 159 f., *KAI*,
No. 214). The location of the two place-names Biq'at Awen and
Beth-'Eden is uncertain. בִּקְעָה (from בקע 'cleave') is used of a
broad ravine or valley. Since the word is used of Coele-Syria, the
valley between Lebanon and the Antilebanon (see Josh. 11.17),
which the Arabs call el-Beḳā'a, it is not improbable that its location is to be sought in this valley. It is, however, doubtful whether
it can be identified with Baalbek, which lies in this valley. It has
been adduced in support of this view that Baalbek in Greek and
Roman writers is called Heliopolis, and that the LXX here reads
Ὦν, which is also the name of the Egyptian Heliopolis (see Gen.
41.45; 46.20, cf. Jer. 43.13). Like the Egyptian city On (אֹן),
which is wrongly vocalized as אָוֶן in Ezek. 30.17, the Aramaic On
will have been altered to אָוֶן in Amos to give the meaning 'valley
of emptiness' (cf. Hosea's alteration of Bethel to Beth-awen in
Hos. 4.15). The uncertainty in this chain of evidence lies partly in
the fact that the LXX reading Ὦν cannot be taken as evidence
that the city of Baalbek was called On (the LXX may have
simply read the consonants with the wrong vowels), and partly
in the fact that we have no evidence that the sun-worship of

Baalbek goes back to the time of Amos. It may therefore be
another city in this valley, whose name Amos intentionally distorts. In that case we cannot recover what the original name was.
בֵּית עֶדֶן, literally 'house of delight' (עֶדֶן vocalized with seghol in
the first syllable to distinguish it from עֵדֶן, the name of the garden
of Paradise, Gen. 2.8), is taken by some to be identical with Bît-
Adini, the Assyrian name for an Aramaean area on the Upper
Euphrates. It would, however, fit better to have a locality which
lay considerably nearer, and Bît-Adini may have already been in
Assyrian possession at the time of Amos; but the suggestions
which have been made of other localities are all dubious (see
Driver's appended note on Eden in his commentary *ad loc.*,
pp. 223 ff.). A few commentators therefore approach the problem quite differently and regard both Biqʿat Awen and Beth-
ʿEden as poetic periphrases for Damascus. But this solution is not
advisable, since we have nothing to suggest that Damascus was
called by these names. גָּלָה (1) 'uncover' (2) 'go into exile' (and
so here). The verb is put in the plural with a subject (עָם) which is
plural in sense (Gr. § 145a–c). Ķir is mentioned as the original
home of the Aramaeans in 9.7. It is also listed together with Elam
and Syria in Isa. 22.6. Some would find it in the vicinity of the
river Ķur, which flows out into the Caspian Sea to the north of
Armenia. But its name is not written with an emphatic *k* in
Assyrian, and this region is not likely to have belonged to the
Assyrian empire at this time. The name cannot therefore be
located more exactly.

According to 2 Kgs. 16.9 the threat of the deportation of the
Aramaeans to Ķir came to fulfilment not many years later. The Aramaean king Rezin had attempted together with Pekah of Israel to
compel king Ahaz of Judah to join a coalition against the Assyrian
king Tiglath-Pileser. Ahaz requested help from Tiglath-Pileser, and
Damascus was captured in 732. The mention of the deportation to
Ķir in the book of Kings may, of course, since it is missing in the
LXX, be dependent on the passage in Amos. But the capture of the
city and the deportation of its inhabitants are in any case quite certain (cf. Tiglath-Pileser's annals in *AOT*, pp. 346 f. and *ANET*,
pp. 282 f.).[1]

[1] It is a misunderstanding of prophecy to use the later fulfilment of prophecies as a
measure of their true value. Nothing was further from the minds of the Old Testament
prophets than to lay stress on a close correspondence between their words and the later

Vv. 6–8: The threat against the Philistines

This people, which dwelt to the west of Judah along the coast of the Mediterranean, came to Palestine somewhat later than the invasion of the land by the Israelites under Joshua, i.e. shortly after 1200 B.C. Their original home is described in the Old Testament as Caphtor (Amos 9.7; Deut. 2.23; Jer. 47.4), which is the Egyptian name for Crete. The name of David's bodyguard הַכְּרֵתִי וְהַפְּלֵתִי (2 Sam. 8.18, etc.) has also been taken as evidence of a connection with the name Crete. It is, however, uncertain whether the Philistines did come from here. Caphtor is better regarded as a name for the cultural world of the Aegean in a wider sense, and their place of origin must be sought in Asia Minor. It is interesting that the LXX translates Caphtor by Cappadocia. They belonged therefore to a completely different race from the Israelites, and differed from them in religion and customs. For example, unlike the Israelites they were not circumcised (1 Sam. 17.36). On Egyptian reliefs they can be easily recognized by their profiles and distinctive head coverings (see the pictures in *AOB*, nos. 11 and 14, *ANEP* 7). Their five cities, Gaza, Ashkelon, Ekron, Ashdod and Gath, each had their own minor princes (1 Sam. 5–6). In the period of the Judges they attacked Israel continuously, and were so superior to them in might that Israel had to introduce the monarchy to ensure its continued existence as a nation. David succeeded in bringing them to their knees, but they were never completely subdued, and from time to time they seized their opportunity to attack Israel throughout the period of the kings. According to 1 Kgs. 15.27 f. king Nadab was slain while he was besieging the Philistine city Gibbethon.

Of the five cities Gath is the only one which is not mentioned. It has been suggested that this is because it was in ruins at this time, Hazael having besieged and conquered it (2 Kgs. 12.18). If Hazael destroyed it it must have been rebuilt, since Sargon conquered it again in 711, and Amos speaks of it himself as an existing city in 6.2. It is therefore most probably an accident that it is not mentioned here, or it may be included in the 'remainder of the

---

course of events. The description just given of the fate of Syria is only undertaken for historical reasons, not as a check of the truthfulness of the prophecy, and the same is true of subsequent notes on the later history of the other peoples.

Philistines' in v. 8. Other commentators conclude from the omission of Gath that the whole passage about the Philistines is secondary. The other four cities of the Philistines, but not Gath, are still mentioned as late as the Books of the Maccabees. This has therefore been taken as evidence that the author lived at a later time when Gath had long been in ruins. The insertion of the threat against the Philistines would then be only a reflection of the view that this could not have been omitted when it is present in so many other passages in the Old Testament where threats are directed against all Israel's neighbours (Isa. 14.29 ff.; Jer. 25.20; 47; Ezek. 25.15–17). There is, however, no convincing evidence against the authenticity of the passage in these objections, while it would have been very strange if Amos himself had not included the Philistines in his threats against the surrounding peoples.

V. 6. Gaza is the largest and most important of the Philistine cities, and can therefore be singled out as the one which bears the most guilt for the offences of the Philistines (cf. above on Damascus). It was the southernmost of the five cities. It lay a little way in from the sea on the main route from Egypt to Mesopotamia. Inland routes went from it to Judah (to the cities of Hebron, Jerusalem and Jericho) and Transjordan and further south to Petra and the coastal cities on the Gulf of Akaba, where there were connections to Arabia. It was therefore an important centre of trade, where caravans from many countries could be encountered. According to Amos, however, this position was misused shamelessly for a slave trade in Israelites, whom the Philistines kidnapped and sold to the Edomites, Israel's neighbours to the south (see further on v. 11). In this way the Israelites could be sold as slaves to the Edomites, or they could sell them again to yet more distant lands. Probably what is in mind here is not prisoners of war (who according to the customs of the time were sold as slaves), but that the Philistines made raids on Israelite territory in times of peace, carried off the populations of entire cities and sold them to the Edomites.

עַל־הַגְלוֹתָם גָּלוּת שְׁלֵמָה literally 'because they have carried off a complete carrying off', i.e. 'because they have carried off the entire population of cities'. גָּלוּת is both abstract and concrete: 'carrying off' and 'those carried off'. According to Joel 4.4–6 the Philistines also sold the Jews as slaves to the Greeks. This perhaps points to a later date.

V. 7. The city, like all the more important cities, was surrounded by a city wall. חוֹמָה is used primarily of a defensive wall
in contrast to גָּדֵר of a wall in general. The punishment is expressed in similar terms to those in v. 4.

V. 8. The first half-verse uses the same expression as occurs in
v. 5. Ashdod (the present-day Eṣdūd) lies about thirty kilometres
north of Gaza on the main road, and like it is a little way from the
coast. Ashkelon (now ʿAṣkalān) lies about thirteen kilometres
south of Ashdod right on the Mediterranean, so that it had connections with the Greek world by sea. הֵשִׁיב יָד עַל 'to bring the
hand back against' means to stretch one's hand out with hostile
intent against; the original meaning 'again' or 'back' which the
verb שׁוּב has is here weakened (cf. Isa. 1.25; Jer. 6.9). Ekron (perhaps the present-day ʿĀḳir) lies about twenty kilometres north-
east of Ashdod, so somewhat further inland than the first three
cities mentioned. In the city there was a temple of the god Baal
Zebub, whom king Ahaziah had consulted when he was seriously
injured as the result of a fall (2 Kgs. 1.2). שְׁאֵרִית פְּלִשְׁתִּים 'the rest
of the Philistines' may either mean the other Philistines apart
from those already mentioned (cf. Jer. 39.3) or more probably
what remains after the devastations just described (cf. 5.15; 9.12
and the similar expression אַחֲרִיתָם 9.1). In either case the sense is
that the Philistines will perish to the last man. Amos concludes
his threat by emphasizing that he has received the words from
Yahweh himself. He uses the expression 'the Lord Yahweh', the
title which he most frequently employs for Yahweh (in all
twenty times).

The threats against the Philistines were partially fulfilled. In
2 Kgs. 18.8 we are told that Hezekiah smote them as far as Gaza, and
2 Chr. 26.6 f. tells of a campaign of Uzziah in which he broke down
the city walls of Gath and Ashdod. How much historical material
there is in these reports is an open question. On the other hand the
Philistines suffered the same fate as all Palestine when the armies of
the Assyrian kings overran the country. Gaza was conquered by the
Assyrians in 732 and 720 (see *AOT*, pp. 347 ff. and *ANET*, pp.
283 ff.), but it was not destroyed, for we hear of it again during
Sennacherib's campaign in 701. It still existed at the time of the
Maccabees (see 1 Macc. 11.61 f.) and in the time of the New Testament (see further on this and the other Philistine cities the articles in

BRL or *IDB*). Ashdod was conquered by Sargon in 711 (*AOT*, pp. 350 f. and *ANET*, pp. 284 f.), but not destroyed. Jeremiah speaks of 'the remnant of Ashdod' (Jer. 25.20), in Nehemiah's time we hear of Ashdodites (Neh. 4.7), and the city is also referred to in 1 Macc. 10.78 ff. Ashkelon was captured by Tiglath-Pileser in 733 and by Sennacherib in 701 (*AOT*, pp. 347 and 353, *ANET*, pp. 283 and 287). The city of Ekron held aloof from attempts at rebellion against the Assyrians until Hezekiah's coalition about 702; it was severely punished by Sennacherib (*AOT*, p. 353, *ANET*, p. 287). It was still of importance in the time of the Maccabees (1 Macc. 10.89).

Vv. 9–10: The threat against Tyre

The threat is directed against Tyre, but applies to the Phoenicians as a whole. These were Israel's neighbours to the north. In Akkadian texts Phoenicia is called *Kinaḫḫi* 'land of purple', a title which was later transferred to Palestine in the form *Kanaʿan*. The Phoenicians inhabited a line of cities on the coast of the Mediterranean: Tyre, Sarepta, Sidon, Gebal, etc. Tyre was the most important of them in the time of Amos. It lay farthest to the south, about fifty kilometres north of Mount Carmel, and was by nature an extremely strong fortress, since it originally stood on an island. This was joined to the mainland with a narrow embankment by Alexander the Great when he was besieging the city. It made its living by trade on land and on sea. Its ships journeyed to the far coasts of the Mediterranean, and brought home great riches (Isa. 23; Ezek. 27). When the Assyrians imposed a tribute on the city at the end of the ninth century B.C., many of the inhabitants emigrated, and founded the 'New City' (Carthage).

In the earliest period the relations between the Phoenicians and Israel were friendly. King Hiram of Tyre sent David cedar wood and craftsmen to build a house for him (2 Sam. 5.11); perhaps this was in effect a form of tribute, since David's census too extended as far as Tyre (2 Sam. 24.6 f.), although Hiram did not lose his independence. Hiram also delivered large quantities of material and men for Solomon's great building operations (1 Kgs. 5.15 ff.; 7.13 ff.), but his position seems to have been significantly stronger than in relation to David, because Solomon in return surrendered twenty towns in Galilee (1 Kgs. 9.11 ff.). Ahab's marriage with Jezebel, a daughter of king Ethbaal of Sidon, is also an expression of the close relationship between the two peoples. This, however, led also to special treatment in Israel for the cult of Baal, to the great indignation of the prophets of Yahweh, who fought against it (1 Kgs. 16.29 ff.). The Phoenicians, like all the inhabitants of Canaan, were Baal worshippers, as has been confirmed by the excavations at Ras Shamra, the ancient Ugarit. This city, which can be regarded as the most northerly of the larger Phoenician cities, lay about 350 kilometres north of Tyre, that is, level with the eastern tip of Cyprus.

Among the texts brought to light at Ras Shamra, which for the most part come from about 1400 B.C., the so-called Keret legend has attracted special attention because of the interpretation of it by its first editor Virolleaud (*La légende de Keret, roi des Sidoniens*, Paris 1936). He claimed that it contained much information about the oldest history of the Phoenicians, and their earlier occupation of southern Palestine, from which they emigrated after a great battle. Virolleaud found here a confirmation of Herodotus' statement that the Phoenicians originally dwelt by the Red Sea. On closer study, however, it has become clear that Virolleaud's theories do not hold water. King Keret's title 'the king of the Sidonians' depends on a misreading, and the battles which are spoken of in the text are not historical in the true sense of the word. On the other hand it is of significance to us to note that Keret pays a visit to the sanctuary of Athirat of the Tyrians and the goddess of the Sidonians when he wants to marry a king's daughter whose home is *Udm* (14 (1 K) 197 ff.). If this *Udm* is the same as the Edom of the Old Testament (cf. Akkadian Udûmu), this may reflect some link between the Phoenicians and the Edomites in ancient times; but this identification is contested as strongly by many scholars as it is supported by others (see on this J. Pedersen, 'Die Krt Legende', *Berytus* 6 (1941), pp. 90 ff.).

The language of the Phoenicians was closely related to Hebrew; it is known only from inscriptions, and is found in several dialects. The oldest inscriptions may go back as far as the eleventh century B.C., the latest come from a time near the beginning of our era (see Z. S. Harris, *A Grammar of the Phoenician Language*, New Haven

1936). The language of the Ras Shamra texts shows an older stage than the earliest known Phoenician inscriptions, and is best described as 'Old Canaanite'.

V. 9. The offence which Tyre has committed is strongly reminiscent of that of the Philistines in v. 6, except that it is not said of the Phoenicians that they have carried away people, only that they have handed them over. If this difference has any significance it means that the Phoenicians have not kidnapped free men, but only taken away slaves and sold them to other people. The text does not say of what nationality these slaves were. It is simplest to think of Israelites, whom they sold to the Edomites (cf. v. 6), but Amos would undoubtedly also criticize them if the slaves were from other nations (cf. on 2.1). It depends on what the meaning is of בְּרִית אַחִים. It is simplest to take it as a 'treaty between brothers', and to think of a treaty between the Israelites and Phoenicians, which the latter had broken by selling Israelites as slaves to Edom.[1] Some commentators object to this that Israel did not feel itself related to the Phoenicians (Gen. 10.15 traces the descent of Sidon from Ham), and that the treaty which was concluded between Solomon and Hiram (1 Kgs. 5.26) certainly resulted in the two kings being called brothers (cf. 1 Kgs. 9.13, cf. 20.32), but could not have this effect in respect of the two peoples as a whole more than two hundred years later. It has therefore been suggested that this refers to a treaty with other Phoenician cities, which Tyre had broken (nothing is known, however, of such a treaty), or to a treaty between Israel and Edom. In that case the meaning would be that the brotherhood between Israel and Edom should have prevented the Phoenicians from selling Israelite slaves to their 'brothers', the Edomites. If this was the sense, however, the offence of the Phoenicians would be subordinate to that of the Edomites, so that it would be difficult to say that the Phoenicians had forgotten the 'treaty of brothers'. The first interpretation of the expression remains therefore the most probable, the reference being to the relationship of friendship which had existed since the time of David and Solomon between the two peoples, and which had also been strengthened in the time of Ahab by his marriage to Jezebel.

---

[1] Cf. with this Joel 4.6, which tells how Tyre and Sidon and the Philistines sold men of Judah and Jerusalem to the Greeks (see on v. 6). Ezek. 27.13 also speaks of trading in slaves: Tyre has traded with Greeks and others, and received slaves in exchange.

בְּרִית 'covenant' or 'treaty', i.e. a mutual relationship between two parties, with the rights and obligations resulting from it. It is a central concept in the Old Testament, with many different shades of meaning, depending on whom the covenant is between (whether it is between men, or between God and men), and whether most emphasis is laid on the obligations, so that the covenant becomes like a sort of law, or whether the promise is predominant, so that the word is close in meaning to grace or promise (see further on this question the standard works on the religion of Israel, and the commentaries on Gen. 6.18; 9.8 ff. and 15.1 ff.).

V. 10. The punishment is the same as for Gaza in v. 7.

Many commentators find the similarity between verses 9–10 and the speech against the Philistines inconsistent with Amos' skill in poetic variation, and explain them as inserted by a later scribe, who wanted to introduce a threat against Tyre, which is often threatened in violent words by the prophets (see Isa. 23; Jer. 25.22; Ezek. 26–28; Zech. 9.2 ff.). On the other hand the same commentators assert that the divergent strophe formation in verses 9–10 in relation to the threats against Damascus and Gaza is also an argument against their genuineness. It may be remarked that it would be more surprising not to find a threat against Tyre, since Amos with conscious effect first directs his utterances against all Israel's neighbours, before he comes to Israel itself. The slight variation in expression in relation to verses 6 ff. is not a serious objection to the genuineness of the passage, since many phrases recur in all the threats in 1.3–2.6. Finally it is a bad principle to lay down rules for what verse patterns and strophe formations Amos could have used. He varies the verses freely as he wishes to, and not according to the rules of European metre.

The threat against Tyre only came to fulfilment much later. The city paid tribute to several Assyrian kings (Hiram of Tyre to Tiglath-Pileser, and a later king of Tyre to Esarhaddon, see *AOT*, p. 357, *ANET*, p. 291), and was also besieged, but never conquered before Alexander the Great, who captured the city in 332 B.C. after a lengthy siege, and had thirty thousand of the inhabitants sold as slaves. It recovered, however, as a trading city (cf. Matt. 11.21 f.; 15.21; Acts 12.20; 21.3, 7) and continued until A.D. 1291, when it suffered its last blow with the Saracen conquest.

Vv. 11–12: Against Edom

East of the depression which runs from the southern point of the Dead Sea to the gulf of Akaba dwelt the Edomites. Israel's view of this people is expressed in the narratives in Genesis which make Esau and Jacob twins, who were already quarrelling in their mother's womb, and as adults lived in so strained a relationship after Jacob's repeated deceptions of his brother that Jacob had to flee from him, and could only keep his freedom by using all his ingenuity when he met his brother on his return from his stay with Laban (Gen. 25.22 ff.; 27; 33). The historical facts are that David subdued the Edomites and put garrisons into the land (2 Sam. 8.13 f., cf. 1 Kgs. 11.15 f.).[1] Israel was from then on the master of Edom until the rebellion under Joram about 850 (2 Kgs. 8.20–22). Amaziah inflicted a serious defeat on Edom and conquered the city of Selaʿ (2 Kgs. 14.7). His son Uzziah fortified the port of Elath and reunited it with Judah. It can be assumed therefore that Judah had recovered control over the trade route to the Gulf of Akaba. But its position cannot have been strongly consolidated in Edom, since 2 Kgs. 16.6 tells how the king of Edom drove the Judaeans out of Elath during the Syro-Ephraimite war (734), and it remained under Edom subsequently.

V. 11. The Edomites are blamed because they have disregarded their close kinship with Israel and used military power against a brother nation, and furthermore have done this in a horrifying way, showing them no mercy. רֶחֶם 'womb', plural 'bowels', especially as the seat of compassion, cf. Gen. 43.14, 30. For רַחֲמָיו one would expect רְחָמָיו (Gr. § 93l). שִׁחֵת רַחֲמָיו 'destroyed his mercy', i.e. choked back any feelings of compassion for his defeated brother nation. Some commentators take רַחֲמָיו as 'his feeling of kinship', but the existence of this special meaning is uncertain. If the following three words are translated 'and he tore his anger perpetually', they must mean that he destroyed his anger. But this is certainly not what is intended. It gives a possible sense if אַפּוֹ is taken as the subject: 'and his anger tore perpetually'. His anger is then compared with a wild beast (cf. Job 16.9). But in that case the change of subject is a difficulty, because

---

[1] There was a rebellion under Solomon, when Hadad was made king with the help of Pharaoh (1 Kgs. 11.21 f.). Edom's independence, however, was certainly only short-lived.

Edom is the subject of both the preceding and the following verbs. Most commentators therefore make a slight alteration of the text to וַיִּטֹּר 'and he kept' (cf. S, V and Jer. 3.5 and Ps. 103.9); this fits in with the parallel verb שָׁמַר. The massoretic vocalization שְׁמָרָה must be taken as a third person masculine with the third feminine suffix, but written without a mappiq in the ה because of the retraction of the tone. עֶבְרָתוֹ must then be taken as a *casus pendens*, picked up by the following suffix in שְׁמָרָה. But it would be simpler to read as in Jer. 3.5 שָׁמַר לָנֶצַח. Instead of giving up its hate Edom brooded continuously over it, to let it burst out at a suitable opportunity.

V. 12 is formed like v. 4 and v. 7. תֵּימָן is the name of a district in Edom (apparently in the northern part, since in Ezek. 25.13 it is contrasted to Dedan, which is placed in the south-eastern part of Edom), here probably the chief city of this district (cf. Eusebius, *Onomasticon*, Jerome, *Liber interpretationis hebraicorum nominum*, in P. de Lagarde, *Onomastica Sacra*, Göttingen 1870, reprinted Hildesheim 1966, pp. 156 and 260, or in E. Klostermann, *Eusebius Werke* 3.i (in Die Griechischen Christlichen Schriftsteller der Ersten Drei Jahrhunderte), Leipzig 1904, pp. 96 f.) A grandson of Esau bears this name in Gen. 36.11, 15. Several times it is used synonymously with Edom as a name for the people (e.g. Jer. 49.20). Teman was renowned for its wisdom (Jer. 49.7); it is therefore not accidental that Eliphaz, one of Job's friends, is called a Temanite (Job 2.11). Bozrah is an important city in Edom, perhaps indeed the capital (see Gen. 36.33), but the name is also used for a district of Edom (Jer. 49.13) or as a poetic designation for the whole of Edom (Jer. 49.22). The city of Bozrah no doubt stood where Buṣaira (literally 'little Bozrah') now is, about thirty-five kilometres south-east of the Dead Sea.

The threat against Edom is treated by many commentators as coming from the post-exilic period. It is claimed that throughout the period of the monarchy to the time of Amos Israel was in control of Edom, with the exception of quite a short period (see above), and that it would therefore be topsy-turvy to say that Edom had persecuted Israel. On the other hand we know that the Edomites had their revenge with the fall of Jerusalem in 587, and created undying hatred of themselves by the Israelites as a result (Lam. 4.21 f.; Obad. 10–14; Ps. 137.7; Mal. 1.4; Ezekiel 25.12–14; Joel 4.19; Jer. 49.7–22; Isa. 34.5–17). It is thought therefore that the threat in Amos was inserted by someone who knew of the conduct of the Edomites in 587 and did not wish a threat against this people to be lacking in Amos. These objections sound very plausible. But it must not be overlooked that there had been war between Israel and Edom in the last hundred years before Amos, and that it is not impossible that the effects of the rebellion against Joram may have spread to southern Judah, which may have been ravaged by the Edomites. In any case they would hardly have treated the Judaean officials gently during the rebellion, so that there could have been circumstances which would justify Amos in using language like that of these verses. An oracle of judgement against Edom fits in with the pattern of Amos' oracles. The variation in the pattern of strophes in vv. 11–12 is not a criterion against their genuineness (cf. on vv. 9–10).

During the period of Assyria's success the Edomites like many other nations had to pay tribute to Tiglath-Pileser, Sennacherib and Esarhaddon (see *AOT*, pp. 348, 352 n. and 357 n.). There is a reference to their conquest by the Babylonian king Nebuchadnezzar in Jer. 27.3 ff. After the exile the Edomites pressed over to the western side of the Araba depression; their new dwelling place was the later Idumaea, the southern part of Judah (cf. the New Testament), while the Nabataeans advanced into the original Edom from Arabia about 300 B.C. On the Arabian expansion after the death of the Prophet the Edomite cities were destroyed. On the archaeological investigations in Edom see N. Glueck, *The Other Side of the Jordan*, New Haven 1940 (reprinted 1952).

Vv. 13–15: Against Ammon

This people dwelt in the land east of the Jordan, east of the tribal territories of Reuben and Gad, between the rivers of Arnon to the south and Jabbok to the north. The Israelites regarded them as related to themselves, but looked down on them as an inferior people. The story of their origin in Genesis 19.30–38 expresses this by making them like the Moabites the offspring of a union between Lot and his daughters. Through the years Israel had numerous clashes with them. Jephthah won a victory over them in the time of the judges, when they made an attack on the land west of the Jordan (Judg. 10.7–11.33). Saul demonstrated his worthiness for the position of king of Israel by defeating them while they were besieging Jabesh in Gilead (1 Sam. 11). Under David they were punished more thoroughly than ever before (2 Sam. 8.12; 10–12), but they were not exterminated as a people, and harried the Israelites in the land east of the Jordan whenever the opportunity arose. They were, however, allied to Ahab at the battle of Qarqar in 853 B.C.

V. 13. Their offence consists in their having tried to exterminate all the Israelites they could by cutting open the wombs of pregnant women, and slaying children in their mother's womb. These expressions should undoubtedly be understood quite literally, since they are in keeping with what is reported in other passages of the Old Testament (2 Kgs. 8.12; 15.16, cf. Hos. 14.1) and in Arabic sources (cf. Wellhausen *ad loc.*, pp. 70 f.). The infinitive בִּקְעָם is formed with *i* for *ŏ* (*u*) in the first syllable (Gr. § 61a). Amos treats these offences as particularly serious because they are not dictated by the rules of war, but quite simply spring from a desire to expand the frontiers of Ammon.

V. 14. The punishment is formulated in phrases similar to those in vv. 4, 7, 10 and 12, only with the verb יצת 'kindle' instead of שלח 'send'. For the assimilation of י to צ in the form הִצַּתִּי see Gr. § 71. רַבָּה or רַבַּת בְּנֵי עַמּוֹן 'Rabbah of the Ammonites' (literally 'the great', i.e. city) is the capital of Ammon (2 Sam. 11.1; 12.26 f.; Deut. 3.11 etc.). After the Arabian conquest of the land it got the name Ammān, which it still has to this day (on the excavations in the city see *BRL* s.v. Rabbat Ammon, cols. 432–435, and *IDB*, s.v. Rabbah, vol. 4, pp. 1 f.). תְּרוּעָה 'cry' is used especially of the war-cry which is raised when the troops charge forward (cf. the corresponding verb רוע in the hiphil, Josh. 6.5; 1 Sam. 4.5). סַעַר 'storm' and סוּפָה (from the root סוּף) '(devastating) storm wind' are both images which express how everything is swept away before the enemy as he charges forward shouting.

V. 15. The Ammonites were ruled by a king (cf. 2 Sam. 10.1), who was to go into exile when punishment came, together with his principal officials שָׂרָיו. גּוֹלָה (1) 'deportation' (2) a collective 'those deported'. Both meanings would fit here. The verse occurs again in a prophecy against Ammon in Jer. 49.3, except that in addition to the leading men there are mentioned also כֹּהֲנָיו 'his priests'. The ancient translations of Jeremiah read instead of

מַלְכָּם 'their king' מִלְכֹּם 'Milcom', the name of the god of the Ammonites (see 1 Kgs. 11.5). In Amos this vocalization fits less well, because כֹּהֲנָיו 'his priests' is lacking in the second half-verse.

Threats against Ammon are found several times in the prophets after Amos, and witness to the resentment Israel constantly bore to this people (Jer. 49.1 ff.; Ezek. 21.33; 25.1 ff.; Zeph. 2.8 f.).

The Ammonites paid tribute to the Assyrian kings Tiglath-Pileser, Sennacherib and Esarhaddon (*AOT*, pp. 348, 352 n. and 357 n.). This did not prevent the Ammonites from making attacks on Judah. In the time of Jehoiakim Judah was ravaged by marauding bands of Moabites and Ammonites (2 Kgs. 24.2). We hear of Ammonites occasionally in the post-exilic period too (Neh. 2.10; 3.35, 41).

CHAPTER TWO

Vv. 1–3: Against Moab

The land of the Moabites lay east of the Dead Sea, with the Edomites as neighbours to the south and the Ammonites to the north-east. The river Arnon formed the northern border with Israel, but this frontier was not a firm one. Before the Israelite invasion from the wilderness the king of the Amorites, Sihon, had wrested from the Moabites the districts north of the Arnon, and when the Israelites slew Sihon and invaded his land they also became masters of this ancient Moabite territory (Num. 21.21–31). Balak king of the Moabites tried in vain to get Balaam to curse Israel and to stop their advance; on the other hand the Moabite women led the Israelites astray (Num. 22 ff.). With the division between the tribes the kingdom of the Amorites fell to Gad, Reuben and Manasseh (Num. 32.33 ff., cf. Josh. 13.15 ff.); they had difficulty, however, in holding the land against the attacks of the Moabites. In the period of the judges Israel was oppressed by Eglon king of Moab, who exacted tribute from them; after eighteen years he was murdered by Ehud (Judg. 3.12 ff.). David in his freebooter period was on good terms with the Moabites, and kept his parents in safety with them (1 Sam. 22.3 f.); as king

he defeated them and made them tributary (2 Sam. 8.2). Probably
the Israelite suzerainty was not of long duration, and may have
been already lost under Solomon or upon his death. In any case
the Book of Kings tells that Mesha king of Moab rebelled against
the king of Israel after the death of Ahab (2 Kgs. 1.1; 3.4 f.), and
that king Joram of Israel and king Jehoshaphat of Judah made an
unsuccessful attempt to subdue the Moabites again (2 Kgs. 3.6–
27). Probably the Moabites were first driven back with Jeroboam
II's victory in the land east of the Jordan (2 Kgs. 14.25). The
summary notice in the Old Testament of Moab's revolt after the
death of Ahab is supplemented and in part corrected by the inscription on the so-called Mesha stone, which was found at
Diban (the Dibon of the Old Testament) in 1868. King Mesha
tells in this inscription, which dates from about 850 B.C., of the
Moabites' sufferings under Omri king of Israel, and how they
rebelled against his son (i.e. Ahab), and completely defeated the
Israelites (see *NSI*, pp. 1 ff.; *KAI*, No. 181). The language of the
inscription shows only insignificant variations in relation to the
Hebrew of the Old Testament. The Old Testament also makes
the two peoples physically related by tracing the Moabites like the
Ammonites back to Lot (cf. on 1.13). A more favourable view of
the relationship of the Moabites to Israel is found in the book of
Ruth, which ends with the Moabite woman Ruth becoming the
mother of David's grandfather (Ruth 4.13 ff.).

V. 1. The offence of the Moabites consists in a profanation of
graves. In ancient times much importance was attached to the
dead man being borne to the family burial place, so that he could
be 'gathered to his fathers' and find rest in the grave. Grave-
robbing, and the disturbance of graves, were regarded as offences
of the lowest nature. Many of the tomb inscriptions that have survived of the Phoenicians and other peoples for this reason utter
violent curses against anyone who should dare to open the grave
(see *NSI*, pp. 26 f., 30 f.; *KAI*, Nos. 13 and 14). Here Amos re-
proaches the Moabites because they have burnt the bones of the
king of Edom to ashes (literally to lime שִׂיד, cf. Isa. 33.12) to
obliterate all traces of them. We do not know what occasion is
referred to, but the meaning is obviously that the Moabites in
some war against Edom drove back their opponents on to their
own territory, opened the royal graves and burnt the bones, and
scattered the ashes to the winds (cf. Jer. 8.1 f.).

It was the custom in Israel to burn bodies only in cases of especially serious offences, where it was impossible to regard the simple death penalty as adequate punishment (the theft of Achan, Josh. 7.15, 25; certain sexual offences, Lev. 20.14; 21.9; Gen. 38.24).[1]

In behaving thus to the Edomites the Moabites treated their king as one would treat a dangerous criminal. It is striking that Amos here attacks the Moabites for an offence that they have committed not against Israel but against another nation. This shows that Yahweh in Amos' view takes displeasure in every offence, wherever it is committed, and that his power was not thought to be confined to Israel, but that he could punish offenders throughout the whole world (cf. 9.1 ff.).

V. 2. For the punishment in the first half-verse cf. 1.4, 7 etc. קְרִיּוֹת is an important city, perhaps even the capital of Moab. It is mentioned in the Old Testament only here and in Jer. 48.24, 41, but occurs also on the Mesha stone (l.13). From this reference it appears that in the city there was a sanctuary of Chemosh, the chief God of the Moabites (see Num. 21.29; 1 Kgs. 11.7). The city is not to be identified with the present Ḳurēyāt (north-west of the old Dibon), which is no doubt the ancient Kiriathaim (Gen. 14.5). We would expect a city in Moab proper. Strangely the name of the city does not occur among the many Moabite cities which are mentioned in Isa. 15–16. This could suggest that it was identical with 'Ar, the first city which is listed in Isa. 15.1 (cf. Num. 21.28, 15), so that the city would have had both these names. If קִיר־מוֹאָב, which is mentioned in Isa. 15.1 in the parallel half-verse, is a proper name, it is perhaps the same as Kerioth, but the expression can also be taken as a collective, 'the cities of Moab'. The second half-verse describes how Moab will perish in the tumult of war (שָׁאוֹן), while the war-cries (cf. 1.14) ring out

---

[1] When Josiah in the course of his reformation had bones from graves burnt on the altar in Bethel, this was not primarily thought of as a punishment for the dead, but as a profanation of the altar (2 Kgs. 23.16, 20). In 1 Sam. 31.12 f. the burning of the bodies of Saul and his sons is of course not a punishment, but to be understood as a purification after the Philistines' treatment of the bodies; after this the bodies were buried in the normal way. In general cremation was not used anywhere in Syria or Palestine, apart from isolated instances from the New Stone Age which have been discovered in Gezer and Jerusalem (see R. A. S. Macalister, *The Excavation of Gezer*, London, 1912, I, pp. 74 f., 285 f., and perhaps also in Jerusalem, see J. G. Duncan, 'Fourth Quarterly Report on the Excavation of the Eastern Hill of Jerusalem', *Quarterly Statement of the Palestine Exploration Fund*, 1924, pp. 166 f.).

and the horns sound. שׁוֹפָר is the curved ox horn or ram's horn.
It is used as a signalling horn, for example as here to sound the
attack (cf. Judg. 3.27), or to sound the alarm (see on 3.6). Sometimes it is also used in the cult for the proclamation of feast-days
(Ps. 81.4; Lev. 25.9). For this, however, use is made more often
of the straight metal instrument חֲצוֹצְרָה, which is usually translated 'trumpet' (Num. 10.2; 2 Kgs. 12.14; 1 Chron. 13.8). The
reliefs on the Arch of Titus give us a picture of what it looked
like (see I. Benzinger, *Hebräische Archäologie*, ed. 3, Leipzig 1927,
p. 335, and *IDB* s.v. Musical Instruments, vol. 3, pp. 472 ff., and
illus. 85).

V. 3. The rulers and leading men of the people will be exterminated (cf. 1. 5, 8 etc.). The topmost man is not called a king,
but a judge שׁוֹפֵט, the word that is used for the rulers of Israel in
the time before the introduction of the monarchy. Their work is
described by the corresponding verb שׁפט 'to settle legal disputes,
to ensure justice'. Since one of the king's most important tasks in
the most ancient times was to settle legal disputes, the word שׁוֹפֵט
is probably simply used here of the king (cf. Mic. 4.14; Ps. 2.10).
It cannot therefore be used as evidence that Moab had no king at
this time, but was tributary to Israel. The feminine suffixes in
מִקִּרְבָּהּ and שָׂרֶיהָ refer to מוֹאָב, which as a land can be feminine (Gr.
§ 122h), while the suffix in עִמּוֹ is governed by the word שׁוֹפֵט. In
v. 1 and v. 2, however, Moab as a people is masculine. There is no
compelling reason to alter the suffixes in v. 3 everywhere to the
masculine.

Moab like Ammon had to pay tribute to the Assyrian kings
Tiglath-Pileser, Sennacherib and Esarhaddon (see above). Threats
against Moab are found also at other places in the prophets, where
judgement is proclaimed against Israel's neighbours (see Isa. 15–16;
Jer. 48; Ezek. 25.8–11, cf. Zeph. 2.8 f.).

Vv. 4–5: Against Judah

Before Amos comes to his real subject he directs his threats
against the kingdom of Judah. For his listeners this must have
been a hint that next time it would be their turn.

V. 4. The declaration of punishment on Judah is constructed

on a different pattern from the others. This is connected with the
special relationship in which Judah stood to Yahweh. Their sin
has therefore appeared in different but certainly no less serious
areas. Judah's sin is first given in general terms: they have despised the law of Yahweh and his commandments. תּוֹרָה 'law' is a
comprehensive term for the will of Yahweh as it is known through
his revelation to men who can communicate it, i.e. priests and
prophets. The word is most frequently derived from the root ירה
'throw'. The thought is of the revelation the priests divined when
they cast lots (Deut. 33.8). Some scholars, however, treat the
word as derived from an Akkadian word *têrtu*, which means
'oracle', 'omen'.[1] In either case the word can be a name for the
revelation which the priests transmit and share with lay people
(see Lev. 10.11; Deut. 17.8 ff.; Hagg. 2.11 ff.; Mal. 2.7). We
must suppose that the oracles which the priests had given at the
temples were passed on (whether orally or in writing), so that one
could at any time draw knowledge from this collection. Guidance
could also be sought from the prophets, because a definite group
of prophets had a firm link with the cultic centres, like that of the
priests. The prophets therefore also use the word תּוֹרָה of Yahweh's revelation to them (Isa. 1.10; Jer. 6.19; Zech. 7.12). The
content of the law (תּוֹרָה) is religious, moral and juridical prescriptions. The individual commandments and prescriptions of
the law are called עֵדֹת, חֻקִּים, מִצְוֹת, דְּבָרִים or מִשְׁפָּטִים, which all have
roughly the same meaning. It was only much later that the mean-
ing of תּוֹרָה was expanded to include all the revelations communi-
cated by Moses, i.e. the Law of Moses. Here the word is used
more generally of Yahweh's revelation, irrespective of whether it
is written down or not. חֹק (from חקק, literally 'carve', sc. on a
tablet or the like, so 'determine', 'decree') is used of the individual commandments of the law (cf. above). In the last line of
the verse it is stated more precisely in what their sin consisted:
they have taken to their fathers' worship of other gods. התעה,
literally 'lead astray from the right way', here in a transferred
sense: 'entice away from the will of Yahweh'. The thought of the
fathers' worship of other gods is also found in later prophets
(Jer. 2.5; 14.20; Ezek. 16). כִּזְבֵיהֶם 'their lies' (from כָּזָב 'lie') is a
circumlocution for their false gods, in contrast to Yahweh as the

---

[1] G. Östborn, *Tōrā in the Old Testament*, Lund, 1945, treats 'showing the way' as the
basic meaning of the word.

true God. The foreign cult is mentioned in such general phrases that we cannot tell what is being referred to. Perhaps it is the Baal cult, with reference to the worship of the golden calf (Exod. 32) or the apostasy to Baal Peor (Num. 25). הלך אחרי 'to go after' is often used of worshipping a god (e.g. Deut. 4.3; 8.19). The expression perhaps means originally 'to follow the image of a god in cult processions'.

V. 5. The punishment will be the destruction of Jerusalem (cf. above on the other cities). The threat was not fulfilled until 587, when Nebuchadnezzar conquered Jerusalem and set fire to the temple, the royal palace and all the houses of the city (2 Kgs. 25.9).

The genuineness of the saying is contested by the great majority of more recent commentators. The objection is made against these verses that the sin for which Judah is reproached is not something concrete, but is expressed in general terms as contempt for the law of Yahweh and his commandments, and the worship of other gods. In this it is claimed the verse shows the influence of Deuteronomy, which has a preference for the use of the words תּוֹרָה and חֻקִּים (4.44 f.; 17.19), of the phrase הלך אחרי in a religious significance (4.3; 6.14; 8.19) and the verb שמר (*passim*). It is further argued that the prophet is not otherwise concerned with Judah in his utterances, and that the surprise of his move to speaking against Israel itself would have been weakened and anticipated if he had first spoken against the neighbouring kingdom in the south, so that they would suspect what was coming. This last argument has little to be said for it. The prophet first, as was the custom of the prophets of success (i.e. prophets who to please the people only foretold good fortune and not judgement), captures the attention of his listeners through hurling threats against a neighbouring people; but after the surrounding peoples had had their turn, it will have awoken mixed feelings among the listeners, and made them wonder when he would stop. When he swooped down on Judah, in spite of all their ill-will to their brother nation in the south they could not have felt malicious pleasure at this, because they would be gripped by a foreboding that it would be their own turn next time. It is no cause for surprise that Amos either does not mention Judah elsewhere at all, or does so only rarely (see 6.1 and 9.11), since his call was to preach to the Northern Kingdom. In the rest of the book threats are not found against the other nations round about which he began his prophetic activity by threatening. Furthermore it must be remembered that neither the threats against the surrounding nations nor those against Judah were expected to be heard by these nations, but by Israel, and if Amos as a Judaean did not spare his own people, the effect on his listeners would be all the stronger. Finally, it is not certain that Amos is dependent on Deuteronomy in these verses. Isa. 5.24b uses almost the same expressions as here. It is also wrong in principle to expect to be able to demonstrate dependence between two writings, when dealing with such common words and phrases, which could be uttered by anyone. The passage in Isaiah is rather evidence that these are words that the prophets have used generally in their preaching.

Vv. 6–16: Against Israel

At last the prophet has come to his proper subject, and is therefore not contented with a summary treatment. After the usual introduction there follows a more detailed description of their offences, which consist in corrupt administration of the law, oppression of the poor, immorality and a degenerate cult (vv. 6–8). Yahweh's kindnesses to the nation have only been rewarded with sin (vv. 9–12). No one will be able to save himself when the punishment comes (vv. 13–16).

V. 6. By 'Israel' the prophet is thinking here of the Northern Kingdom, in contrast to Judah in v. 4. This is not contradicted by the fact that verses 9–11 mention events which according to the tradition the Judaeans also took part in. The word 'Israel' is also used of the Northern Kingdom in 7.8–11, 15–17. In other places, however, Amos uses it in the wider sense of the whole people (see 3.1; 9.7 and 14). For the Northern Kingdom he never uses the name Ephraim, but either Israel or Joseph (5.15; 6.6) or (the house of) Jacob (3.13; 6.8; 9.8) or (the house of) Isaac (7.9, 16).

The prophet begins his oracle against Israel by attacking them for their administration of justice. צַדִּיק means here not the man who is morally unblemished, but the man who has right on his side in a law case (cf. Deut. 25.1). It is the judge's duty to declare righteous (hiphil of the verb צדק) the man who has right on his side, while the man who does not should be condemned (hiphil of רשע). But Amos has to reproach the judges that their judgement has been sold for money, or for as little as a pair of sandals, so that their verdicts have gone against the innocent and poor, who did not have the means to bribe the judge (cf. Isa. 5.23). 'Sell the righteous' is therefore not to be taken literally, but means 'to condemn him for payment'. מִכְרָם has *i* in the first syllable, as does בִּקְעָם in 1.13. כֶּסֶף 'silver' is the most general means of payment; for this reason it comes to mean 'money' (i.e. they had a silver standard). From the parallel נַעֲלַיִם 'a pair of sandals', 'money' must here be understood to be a trivial sum. This is supported by the use of נַעֲלַיִם in 1 Sam. 12.3 (restored on the basis of the LXX) almost proverbially for something trivially cheap. 'בְּ pretii' in the first half-verse is followed by בַּעֲבוּר in the parallel half-verse with the same meaning. Some, however, take בַּעֲבוּר נַעֲלַיִם in another way than בְּכָסֶף, as referring to the principle that a creditor could sell his debtor as a slave, if he could not pay his debts (2 Kgs. 4.1; Lev. 25.39 f.; Matt. 18.25). What is complained of here is then that the creditors have been so hard-hearted that they have sold their debtors, because they were in arrears for as little as a pair of sandals. This interpretation fits the first half-verse less well, however, because the word 'sell' will then be used first in a transferred sense, and then in the literal sense. Furthermore the first instance will then be a question of flagrant violation of the sanctity of the law, while the second instance is only of a hard-hearted, not an absolutely illegal method of procedure. It is a less decisive objection that the subject of the action on this interpretation is no longer the judges but the rich creditors. In v. 8 it is definitely these last that are meant, in v. 7 it is not clear. This is obviously connected with the fact that the judges and the rich joined together to squeeze the poor. They are therefore not sharply separated from one another in the individual expressions. An ingenious but improbable interpretation builds on the possibility that the mention of the sandals may be a reference to the old custom of taking off one's sandals and giving them to the other party for confirmation of a redemption or an exchange (Ruth 4.7). The sandals would in that case signify a conveyance or a mortgage deed, and the meaning be that the judges not only let themselves be bribed with ready money, but with mortgages on the poor men's own property.

V. 7. The first half-verse continues the description of the injustices done to the poor, but the text is very difficult to translate. It has been translated: 'those who seek the dust of the earth on

the head of the poor', and understood as meaning that the poor
did not even have the right to scatter earth on their head when
they mourned, either for their dead or to show their wretchedness
after the corrupt law cases. For the custom of scattering earth on
the head as a sign of mourning see 2 Sam. 1.2; 15.32; Lam. 2.10.
Others understand the expression in a pregnant sense: 'those who
strive to bring the dust of the earth upon the heads of the poor',
i.e. to bring them to sorrow and misery. It is better to take שָׁאַף as
equivalent to שׁוּף 'crush'. The following בְּ can introduce an
object, on the analogy of the verbs פָּגַע and פָּגַשׁ, which sometimes
have the object following directly, sometimes introduced by בְּ.
The translation in that case is: 'Those who crush the head of the
poor in the dust of the earth', a figurative expression for the
treading under foot of the rights of the poor (cf. Isa. 3.15: 'How
can you crush my people and grind the faces of the poor?'). דַּל
literally 'thin' (Gen. 41.19), here 'small', 'poor'. Roughly the
same thought is expressed in 'and they turn aside the way of the
poor'. To turn aside someone's way means to bring him to disaster by persecuting and oppressing him (cf. Job. 24.4). The subject may therefore well be the rich (as in v. 8), but it is also
possible that the poor are not getting the justice that is due to
them from the judiciary, so that the verse is an attack on the
judges (see on v. 7). עָנָו 'humble', is often used in the same sense
as עָנִי 'wretched', as appears from the fact that it can be used as a
parallel to אֶבְיוֹן or דַּל (see Isa. 11.4; 29.19).

7b introduces a reproach of a completely different character.
Here the prophet is lamenting the immorality of the people. The
emphasis is hardly on father and son going into the same maiden
(הנערה with article), so that the prophet is accusing them of in-
cest (Lev. 20.11, cf. 1. Cor. 5.1). The article should be taken
generally, the accusation being directed against the shameless
way in which father and son betake themselves[1] openly and as if
it could be taken for granted to הנערה, which is here used of the
young women who devoted themselves to immorality in the
temples under the influence of the religion of the Canaanites.
It was thought that the young women had a share in promoting
fertility when they prostituted themselves in the service of the
goddess Astarte. The money earned, which went to the temples,

---

[1] הלך, not בוא 'go in', which is used of sexual intercourse, cf. Gen. 16.2; 38.8.

was contemptuously stigmatized by the prophets of Yahweh as 'the hire of harlots' (Hos. 9.1; Mic. 1.7; cf. Deut. 23.18). A woman who devoted herself in this way was called קְדֵשָׁה 'a holy woman', 'a dedicated woman' (cf. Gen. 38.21 f.; Hos. 4.14). This form of cultus had exercised so great an attraction on the Israelites that it won a place in the temples of Yahweh, where both men and women dedicated themselves to it. Even in the temple in Jerusalem there were to be found in the time of Manasseh men who prostituted themselves (2 Kgs. 23.7, cf. 1 Kgs. 14.24; 15.12; 22.47). Amos shrinks from calling these women 'holy', and uses instead the word הנערה. On the contrary he thinks that intercourse with this kind of woman is a profanation of the name of Yahweh. למען should really mean that they did it with definite intent; but it is rather a cutting way for the prophet to express the result of their activity. The root חלל means the opposite of what is holy. The verb חלל in the piel therefore means 'to profane' (cf. חל 'profane'). The intercourse of Israelites with temple prostitutes is contrary to the will of Yahweh, and is a profanation of his holy name. When Yahweh made himself known to Israel and revealed his name, he thereby gave expression to his will and his innermost being. A violation of the will of Yahweh is therefore in effect a profanation of his name. This is even more obvious if temple prostitution has taken place in the sanctuaries which were dedicated to Yahweh (see v. 8).

V. 8. Wild drinking bouts went together with sexual laxity in the cult under Canaanite influence (see Hos. 4.11–14). Here too the rich show how low they have sunk, because these feasts are literally held at the expense of the poor. Perhaps it was already the sense in v. 7b that the payments to the temple prostitutes were extorted from the poor, so that the transition from v. 7a to 7b is not without a link. In any case it emerges clearly in v. 8 that both the cloaks on which they stretched themselves at the immoral parties, and the wine they got drunk on, were obtained by the impoverishment of and distraint on the poor. According to the law (Ex. 22.25 f.; Deut. 24.11–13) cloaks which were taken in pledge (חֲבֻלִים) were not the property of the creditors, but had to be handed back to the debtor before sunset because of the cold of the night. This rule they violated by keeping them during their orgies, which naturally went on till long into the night (cf. Isa. 5.11 f.). בְּגָדִים (plural of בֶּגֶד) refers to the large four-cornered pieces of unsewn material which were used for outer clothing or cloaks (שִׂמְלָה). יַטּוּ here 'spread a bed' (מִטָּה) or perhaps intransitive 'spread oneself', 'stretch oneself'. 'Beside every altar' is meant to indicate how widespread this custom was. יֵין עֲנוּשִׁים 'wine from those fined' either means wine bought with the money collected in fines from the poor, or wine that had been distrained on because the debtor did not have the money to pay. In either case we should perhaps think that the poor were sentenced to these fines in violation of the law by the judges and rich men, so that the prophet means to describe not only their heartlessness, but also the breach of the law which they commit in order to hold their orgies. Fines paid to the state are not known in Israel; they are paid to the injured party (see Ex. 21.22; Deut. 22.19).

בית אלהיהם (accusative of place, Gr. § 118d–g) either 'in the house of their god(s)' or 'in their "god-house"', i.e. in their temple. In the first case it would not be meant that the temples were of Yahweh, but since the prophet would not be so shocked that such things were rife in the temples of other gods, the latter interpretation is preferable. Then the seriousness lies in the fact that it happens in temples which were dedicated to Yahweh. On great festivals in ancient Israel the people gathered at the sanctuaries to offer sacrifice and to take part in the sacrificial feasts, which could be held in a special banqueting-hall which was part of the temple (1 Sam. 9.22, cf. 1.18 according to the LXX, see also Judg. 9.27, where the expression בית אלהיהם is similarly found). Because of the moral degradation of the country the feasts in Amos' time had degenerated in the manner described by the prophet.

V. 9. וְאָנֹכִי comes first for emphasis ('and yet *I* have') to show the glaring contrast between Yahweh's acts of kindness to the people and the sinfulness with which they have so shamefully repaid his care for them. The Amorites are used here as a general name for the pre-Israelite population in the land west of the Jordan (cf. Gen. 48.22; Josh. 24.15; Judg. 6.10; 2 Sam. 21.2). From other passages it appears that the Amorites were only a single tribe within this population who had their home mainly in the mountain districts (Deut. 1.19 f.; Josh. 10.5 f.). Finally Amorites can be used as a name for the population of the two kingdoms of Heshbon and Bashan north of Moab, where Og and Sihon reigned (Num. 21.13; Josh. 24.8). מפניהם literally 'from before them', i.e. the Amorites were driven out, so that they no longer stood in the way of the Israelites. Some commentators read the second person plural suffix as in v. 10, assuming that the reading with the third person has been influenced by v. 8. The Amorites are described as a nation of giants, whom the Israelites could not have defeated without the assistance of Yahweh. This picture of the original population can be compared with the mention of the sons of Anak in Num. 13.32 f. (the Israelites were like grasshoppers in comparison to them, cf. Deut. 1.28).

Cedar trees were for the Israelites the embodiment of height and dignity, as oaks were of strength (cf. Isa. 2.13). חָסֹן 'strong' (only here and Isa. 1.31). אַלּוֹן 'oak'[1]: the oaks of Bashan in particular were famous (Isa. 2.13; Ezek. 27.6). The image of the trees is continued in the mention of fruit and roots. Both of these were destroyed, so that they could neither germinate new trees nor send out fresh shoots from the stump (cf. Ezek. 17.9; Hos. 9.16; Isa. 37.31; Job 18.16 and the Eshmun'azar inscription, lines 11 f., see *NSI*, pp. 30 ff.; *KAI*, No. 14).

V. 10 continues with a mention of Yahweh's kindnesses to the people in the earliest days, with no stress laid on the correct chronological sequence of events (if it were, v. 9 would have to follow after v. 10). The leading out from Egypt[2] and the subsequent events at Sinai formed the highest points in Yahweh's saving wonders towards the people.[3] Nor could the people have come through the period of the stay in the wilderness, where drought, starvation and other hardships threatened, by their own resources (on the thought of the verse cf. Deut. 6.12, and Hos. 13.4 f.). Here the period in the wilderness is a time of grace for the people. In other places, however, the prolonged stay in the wilderness is understood as a punishment for the disobedience of the people (Num. 20.8 ff.; Deut. 1.34 ff.). The number forty is a favourite round number in both the Old and the New Testaments. The rain continued for forty days in Gen. 7.17; Moses'

---

[1] The distinction made by the massoretes between אַלָּה, אַלּוֹן and אֵלָה, אֵלוֹן, which on the basis of the ancient translations are usually rendered respectively by 'oak' and 'terebinth', is artificial. All the words mean originally 'a large tree in which a divinity dwells'. It is is a widespread idea in the ancient Orient that the god is identified with the holy tree.

[2] From the low-lying land of Egypt one goes up (עלה) to Palestine, which is a hilly country; in the opposite direction one goes down (ירד, Gen. 12.10).

[3] The theme of the Exodus is combined in 1 Kgs. 12.28 with the Canaanite-influenced pilgrimage feast.

life falls into three periods of forty years (Acts 7.23; Exod. 7.7;
Deut. 34.7); Elijah is forty days on the way to Horeb (1 Kings
19.8); Jesus fasts forty days (Matt. 4.2) and is seen on earth forty
days after his resurrection (Acts 1.3). אֶרֶץ הָאֱמֹרִי is 'the land of
Canaan'.

V. 11. As the last of Yahweh's kindnesses to the people the
prophets and the Nazirites are mentioned as those who should
give the people spiritual and moral strength. The hiphil of קוּם
'rise up' is used with Yahweh as subject, when he makes men
appear with a special task for the good of the people, whether they
are judges (Judg. 2.16, 18, cf. 3.9, 15), kings (Jer. 23.4 f., 30.9;
Ezek. 34.23), prophets (Deut. 18.15, cf. Jer. 6.17) or priests
(1 Sam. 2.35). מִבְּנֵיכֶם partitive: 'some of your sons'. נָבִיא 'prophet',
i.e. a divinely inspired man who proclaims the message which
he has either seen or heard in his ecstasy. As a rule he is connected with a temple, where he functions as a cult-prophet.[1] In
general he is also a member of a prophetic band under a leader.
The word can be used for both true and false prophets; here of
course it is used with reference to the great prophets of Yahweh
in the past, like Moses, Samuel, Nathan, Gad, Elijah and Elisha
(see further on Amos' conception of the prophets and his use of
the word on 3.7 and 7.14). נָזִיר (from נזר with the basic significance
of 'separate out', 'dedicate') means 'one dedicated'. It is used of
the prince in Gen. 49.26, Deut. 33.16, but otherwise it is used of
the men whom we call 'Nazirites', i.e. men who have dedicated
themselves to Yahweh and pledged themselves to abstain from
wine, avoid contact with corpses and let their hair grow until the
completion of the time for which they have dedicated themselves
(see the law on the Nazirites, Num. 6.1–21). Samson was dedicated already before his birth (cf. John the Baptist, Luke 1.15) for
his whole life (Judg. 13.5, 7; 16.17). He is the only completely
certain example of a Nazirite in the Old Testament, but Samuel
must also probably be understood as one, even though the word
נָזִיר is not used of him (1 Sam. 1.11, 28: he is to let his hair grow,
and is given to Yahweh for his whole life). It may be an accident

---

[1] In many of the other Semitic languages the corresponding verb occurs in the sense of
'appear with a communication', 'proclaim'. The etymology of the word is therefore
quite clear. On the cult-prophets see A. Haldar, *Associations of Cult Prophets among the
Ancient Semites*, Uppsala, 1945; A. R. Johnson, *The Cultic Prophet in Ancient Israel*,
Cardiff, 1944, ed. 2, 1962; and S. Mowinckel, *Kultprophetie und prophetische Psalmen*
(Psalmenstudien III), Christiania, 1923.

that the examples we have are both of men who also had the task
of fighting against the enemies of the people. Otherwise their
abstention from wine reminds us of the Rechabites, whose founder
Jonadab son of Rechab lived at the time of Jehu (2 Kgs. 10.15).
Jeremiah makes special mention of them as a shining example to
the people (Jer. 35). From his mention of them it appears that
they not only rejected the use of wine, but were in reaction against
the whole cultural life of Canaan, and sought to get back to the
simpler life and customs of the past, when men did not live in
houses or till the soil. In a similar way Amos' stress on the Nazirites can be understood as a protest against the sophisticated and
degenerate life of his time, in particular as it appeared in the large
cities. וּמִבַּחוּרֵיכֶם 'and some of your young men' parallel with
'some of your sons' shows that it was especially the young who
were dedicated to special tasks in the service of Yahweh. Surprise
has been felt that Amos does not mention the priests as pillars of
the people. This is possibly connected with his conflict with the
high-priest in Bethel (7.10–17), but could be coincidental.

In the second half-verse the prophet appeals directly to his
listeners, asking them if things are not as he has said, and they
have of necessity to agree that he is right. The final words
נְאֻם־יְהוָה 'it is heard from Yahweh' underline the divine origin of
his words. נְאֻם is the passive participle (used as a noun in the construct with the following word) of a verb which means 'whisper'.
This verb is not otherwise used in Hebrew (with the exception of
Jer. 23.31, where it is derived from the expression נאם־יהוה), but
its meaning is secured from the corresponding verb in Arabic.
The formula נאם־יהוה means therefore 'what is whispered by Yahweh', or 'Yahweh's utterance'. It can be inserted at the beginning
of an utterance, or it can come at the end, as here. The formula
occurs about four hundred times in the prophets, and almost only
in them.

V. 12. The Israelites could not have behaved worse than they
did, because they compelled the Nazirites to break their vows of
abstention from wine, and tried to prevent the prophets from
fulfilling their task as preachers of the words which Yahweh had
inspired them to preach. The prophets felt themselves driven by
an inner compulsion when the spirit of Yahweh came upon them,
and reacted violently if anyone tried to prevent them from
preaching his word (1 Kgs. 22.27; Isa. 30.10 f.; Jer. 11.21; 20.7–

10; Mic. 2.6). Amos himself experienced this when he received his expulsion order because of his preaching. לֹא with the imperfect is used of an absolute prohibition (Gr. § 107 o). The daghesh in תּ is daghesh lene after a disjunctive accent (Gr. § 21a–b).

V. 13. הִנֵּה introduces the judgement, which is described in more detail than after any of the preceding threats. The uncertainty about the meaning of the verb מֵעִיק has produced very different interpretations of the verse. Since the meaning of the root is not certain in Hebrew, recourse has been had to the other Semitic languages to determine it. Some refer to the Arabic ʿāqa (medial waw) 'hamper', 'hinder', and think that העגלה is a threshing cart or a threshing wheel (cf. Isa. 28.27 f.), so that the translation is: 'I let (it) come to a halt beneath you (i.e. where you stand), as a threshing wheel, which is full of straw, comes to a halt'. The sense would be that they will one day 'get stuck', so that they cannot escape Yahweh's punishment. Others suggest the Arabic verb ʿaqqa (ע״ע root), which means 'cut up in pieces': 'I will cut you up in the place where you are, as a threshing cart cuts up', a figurative expression for the way in which they are cut down by enemies. Others again take העגלה as a cart, and work from the Arabic ʿāqa (ע״י root) 'groan': 'I will make it groan beneath you . . .'. It is then assumed that the punishment will affect them in the form of an earthquake. Finally some have taken עוק as an Aramaism (cf. עָקָה Ps. 55.4 and מוּעָקָה Ps. 66.11, both rendered by the LXX with θλίψις) for the Hebrew צוק (hiphil 'press'): 'I will press you etc.'. The meaning in this case is that they will be held fast in their place and not be able to escape. Such an Aramaism at the time of Amos is not very probable, so that it is necessary to consider only the first three suggested meanings. The objection has been made that we have no reason to think that harvest-carts were used in ancient Israel (any more than they are used at the present day among the Arabs in the Near East), but this does not of itself exclude the possibility that Amos may have used this image, if in fact other carts were known in ancient times (Gen. 46.5, 1 Sam. 6.7 ff.). All three suggestions may therefore be regarded as possible, although the first and the second best fit the following verses, which talk of disaster in war. תַּחַת is probably originally a substantive, which signifies 'the under part'; it is used derivatively in the construct as a preposition 'under'. Its original meaning can still be seen here: 'your

underside' means 'the place where you are standing'. לָהּ ethical
dative (Gr. § 119s): 'which is full (for itself) of'. עָמִיר is a collective, and means 'straw' or 'hay' (cf. BDB; KB has 'swath,
row of newly cut grain'). It is rendered in the Revised Version
rather inaccurately by 'sheaves'. The single bound sheaf is in fact
called אֲלֻמָּה* (see Gen. 37.7; Ps. 126.6).

V. 14. After this we are told in detail how the catastrophe
develops. Swiftness is a virtue in a warrior (2 Sam. 2.18 ff.;
Eccles. 9.11), but even the swiftest will not be able to find a place
of refuge, and the strong warrior will not be able to use his
strength, either because he is paralysed by fright or because the
superior force is too crushing. אמץ qal: 'be strong', piel: 'make
strong', with object כֹּחוֹ 'display, use his strength'. גִּבּוֹר 'strong'
is often used of the experienced warrior (1 Sam. 2.4; Isa. 3.2; Ps.
19.6). He too will not escape with his life in the devastating battle.

V. 15. תֹּפֵשׂ הַקֶּשֶׁת 'archer, bowman'. The employment of
archers in the Israelite army was not as common as it was with the
Assyrians and Aramaeans (see *BRL*, cols. 115 f., *IDB*, s.v.
Archer, vol. 1, p. 208). עָמַד here: 'hold one's ground'. After יְמַלֵּט
the word נַפְשׁוֹ can be supplied, or the form can be vocalized as a
niphal. The reference to the rider can be taken as evidence that an
Israelite cavalry existed in the eighth century, but it cannot have
played any important part in the warfare of the time (see *BRL*,
s.v. Pferd, cols. 419–427, *IDB*, s.v. Horse, vol. 2, pp. 646 f.).

V. 16. אַמִּיץ לִבּוֹ 'the strong in respect of his heart', 'the brave'
(for the construct link see Gr. § 128y); in the context of the following 'among the mighty' it acquires a superlative meaning 'the
bravest among the mighty' (Gr. § 133g). עָרוֹם does not necessarily mean naked in the full sense, but can be used of one who has
taken off his outer clothes, and is only dressed in a tunic (1 Sam.
19.24; John 21.7). Perhaps it can also be used of one who has no
weapons (cf. the Targum here). The warriors throw away their
heavy cloaks, or perhaps their weapons, to be able to flee without
impediments. עָרוֹם is an accusative of circumstance (Gr. § 118n).
'On that day' means on the day of misfortune, when the armies
of the enemy inflict a crushing defeat on Israel. Amos does not
mention Assyria explicitly, but it can be concluded from 5.27 that
it must be this people that he thought would perform the punishment.

CHAPTER THREE

After the oracle of punishment against Israel, 2.6–16, there follows in the second main section of the book (chaps. 3–6) a more detailed variation on the basic theme which has already been stated. The section should not be treated as a continuous utterance, but as consisting of larger and smaller passages, which sometimes have only a slight connection with one another.

Vv. 1–2: The election of Israel has given it all the greater responsibility

V. 1. The speech is directed to בני ישראל, by which one could think of the population of the Northern Kingdom, in contrast to בני יהודה. However, the addition which is made in v. 1b shows that the expression is to be understood as referring to the people as a whole. In this connection we must ignore the more recent studies which have established that not all the tribes were in Egypt. On this subject Amos shares the views of his period. The election applies to the nation; therefore the obligations which follow from it are also shared by all Israelites. But Amos' task is especially to castigate the population of the Northern Kingdom, whose falling away was the worst, so that he has them particularly in mind in these words. Only occasionally does he pay special attention to Judah, or include it in his oracles against the sinful nation (cf. on 2.6). In v. 1a the words of Yahweh are reported in the third person, while he is represented as speaking in the first person in v. 1b. Many commentators are dissatisfied with this, and treat v. 1b as an addition. But in doing so they make the unreasonable demand that the prophets in their oracles should attain the precision that we would expect in a carefully revised literary account. מִשְׁפָּחָה 'family' can also, as here, be used of a whole nation (cf. Gen. 12.3; 28.14; Mic. 2.3; Jer. 8.3).

V. 2. The verb יָדַע 'know' contains more than a dispassionate statement of what Israel was. Yahweh has of his own free will cared for Israel and looked after it, so that 'to know' approaches

the sense of 'to choose' (cf. Gen. 18.19; 2 Sam. 7.20; Jer. 1.5
Hos. 13.5). While v. 2a simply expresses the current conception
of Israel's unique position among other nations, v. 2b draws a
completely different conclusion from this than Amos' contemporaries did. It was thought that the special status of the people
would give it security against disaster in all circumstances. If the
Israelites were not unaware that they had broken the commandments of Yahweh in many areas, they always thought that in their
cult they had the means to change Yahweh's mind, so that he
would never make an end of the covenant. Amos goes directly
against this view, and says that it is precisely their special position
that gives them so much the greater obligations than other
nations. His view can perhaps best be paraphrased in the words of
the gospel: 'Every one to whom much is given, of him will much
be required' (Luke 12.48). אֶתְכֶם comes before the verb for emphasis. הָאֲדָמָה not 'the land', but 'the earth'. פָּקַד 'visit', also in a
hostile meaning, 'to afflict, punish' (the person is introduced by
עַל, and the offence appears as the object). עָוֹן 'sin', 'offence'. The
basic meaning of the root is probably 'to turn aside from the
way', 'to go astray' (cf. Arab. ġawā).

Vv. 3–8: A series of examples of the laws of cause and effect, taken from daily life, establishes why the prophet has of necessity to speak as he does

Since Amos' preaching cut across the general outlook of the
people, it was by no means uncalled for that he should give a
justification of his right to appear as the proclaimer of Yahweh's
judgement on the people (cf. vv. 1–2). He refers to the inner
compulsion which comes upon a man when Yahweh reveals
himself to him, and tells him to prophesy; and to convince his
listeners of this, he directs a series of questions to them, all of
which they cannot but answer in the negative. Having conceded
the impossibility of denying the indissoluble connection between
certain well-known phenomena like the roaring of the lion and
his prey, or the fall of a bird to the earth and a throwing stick, they
must also concede a close connection between Amos' preaching,
and Yahweh's command to him to prophesy. The proof is not
compelling according to the demands of Western logic. This is

because in Amos' time more importance was attached to making an impression on the listeners by the use of images and strong words than by proofs in the strict sense. Neither should we object if the prophet in some of the instances that follow concludes from cause to effect, and in others from effect to cause. It is exclusively the connection between the phenomena that he is concerned to emphasize.

V. 3. 'Do two walk together, unless they have made an appointment?' is of course not to be understood as implying that two men cannot meet by accident. But if they walk together along the road, they must have agreed to keep company with one another. Since it can be dangerous in desolate regions to walk together with a person unless he is actually known to one, many prefer the LXX's reading ἐὰν μὴ γνωρίσωσιν ἑαυτούς, which would correspond to נוֹדָעוּ (i.e. interchange of ע and ד). בִּלְתִּי אִם = 'unless'.

V. 4. The questions in the first and second half-verses are not identical. The lion's roar in 4a is the ferocious roar with which the lion throws himself at his prey. When it is heard one can tell that the lion has found his prey (cf. Isa. 5.29; Ezek. 22.25). In 4b, however, it is the contented growl which he utters when he has proudly dragged his prey to his den. יַעַר is here 'scrub'. In other passages the word is used for the forest proper, which is comparatively rare in Palestine. אַרְיֵה 'lion', i.e. the fully-grown lion, in contrast to כְּפִיר 'young lion', which, however, is old enough to go hunting (for a cub the word גּוּר is used). Both examples are intended to show that the roar of the lion always has its cause. The image is not to be interpreted further, with the lion taken as Yahweh, and the prey as Israel, which is carried off. Amos' reference to the lion may point to personal experience from his life as a shepherd. The lion has long been extinct in Palestine.

V. 5. פַּח and מוֹקֵשׁ are two different devices for catching birds. פַּח is a net which collapses around the bird when it touches a tongue in it. Nets of this sort are known from Egyptian pictures (see the reconstruction in *AOB*, illus. 182). מוֹקֵשׁ means according to some a tongue which releases a mechanism in the net, by which the bird is thrown to the ground and caught; according to others it is a throwing-stick (boomerang) which is thrown at the bird. This too is known from Egyptian pictures (see A. Erman and H. Ranke, *Ägypten und ägyptisches Leben im Altertum*, rev. ed.,

Tübingen 1923, p. 264). Perhaps the two methods of capture are mixed together in v. 5a. If the word פַּח is deleted in 5a, as having come into the text by mistake from 5b, where it also occurs after the consonants (ה) עַל, the text becomes easier to understand (cf. the LXX). לָהּ refers to צִפּוֹר, which is feminine, as the verb also shows. The images are not to be allegorized, with the bird as Israel, which is caught by reason of its sin. Amos only means to say that when a bird is caught this has a cause; either it has touched the tongue in a trap, or it has been hit by a throwing-stick.

V. 6. אִם has the same meaning as הֲ in the preceding verse: it implies an answer in the negative. When the trumpet is sounded (see 2.2) one knows that danger is near, and is seized with terror. In this half-verse the conclusion is therefore from cause to effect, in contrast to vv. 3–5. יחרדו is plural after עָם (Gr. § 145a–c). In the second half-verse the conclusion is again drawn from effect to cause. רָעָה here: 'misfortune' (not of moral evil). In ancient times in Israel it was the general belief that disasters also come from Yahweh, who causes all that happens. It is only later that speculations are found whether there are occurrences which are not caused by him (compare the difference between 2 Sam. 24.1 and 1 Chron. 21.1).

Vv. 7–8. Many commentators regard v. 7 as a later addition, intended to give an explanation of vv. 6b and 8b: because Yahweh reveals to the prophets in advance what misfortunes are coming, they can and should speak to the people of them. It is further asserted that the representation of the prophets as the servants of Yahweh only fits the later prophets (Jer. 7.25; 25.4; Ezek. 38.17; Zech. 1.6), and that the expression גָּלָה סוֹד 'reveal a secret' is also late (see Prov. 11.13; 20.19; 25.9). If v. 7 is secondary, the point of the whole passage from v. 3 onwards is that Amos intends to justify his right to appear as a prophet. He does this by pointing out that it is just as impossible to refrain from preaching the word of Yahweh as it is to refrain from being frightened when the lion roars (v. 8). V. 7 can, however, be interpreted as a far from superfluous element in the context. כִּי is then best taken in the sense of 'but' or 'no'. Amos has shown that all disasters are caused by Yahweh, but adds that he first told the prophets of them, so that they could warn the people of what was imminent, and call them to repentance, so that they could avoid punishment. For this reason Amos feels it his duty to warn them, and he can no more refrain from proclaiming Yahweh's word of warning than one can help being afraid when the lion roars. The fact that the representation of the prophets as the servants of Yahweh occurs especially in Jeremiah and the later prophets is not sufficient as proof that Amos could not also have used this image. דָּבָר here 'thing'. The expression should not be pressed; Amos means that Yahweh does nothing of significance without telling the prophets of it. סוֹד can be used of a confidential meeting or a council, but also of the decision which is taken at such a council. For this reason it develops the meaning of 'secret'.

The examples which are given in v. 8 are again from cause to effect.

Vv. 9-15: Foreign nations are called as witnesses to the licentiousness in Samaria (vv. 9-10). After this judgement is proclaimed in varying expressions and images (vv. 11, 12, 13-15)

V. 9. The prophet utters a call to the people in the Philistine town of Ashdod and in Egypt to come here and see the wild and unbridled life that is lived in Samaria. Even these men, who are not regarded as good examples of a moral life, will be shocked at the excesses they will witness. It is not said whom the prophet addresses with the imperative הַשְׁמִיעוּ (and אִמְרוּ in v. 9b). It has been suggested that it is the prophets, or better that the second person plural is indeterminate, corresponding to our 'one'. The book of Deutero-Isaiah is introduced in a similar way with an address to some imaginary messengers (Isa. 40.1). עַל־אַרְמְנוֹת can be interpreted as meaning either that the cry will sound out over the palaces, or that men will cry out standing on the flat roofs of the palaces (cf. Matt. 10.27 κηρύξατε ἐπὶ τῶν δωμάτων). אַרְמְנוֹת בְּ is an example of the employment of the construct state before a preposition (Gr. § 130a). In place of אַשְׁדּוֹד some read with the LXX אַשּׁוּר, as a result of which the parallelism is improved. But the alteration is not necessary. If the plural הָרֵי שֹׁמְרוֹן is read, the sense is that the foreigners will gather on the hills around Samaria (which was surrounded by a circle of higher hills from which one could look down on to the city). The LXX reads the singular, referring to the actual hill on which the city was built. Samaria

was built by Omri, and made the capital of the country (1 Kgs.
16.24). Amos had possibly been in the city (which by Israelite
standards was a large one) himself, and seen the many magnificent
palaces of which excavations on the site have given us some idea.
The walls of the palaces were covered with expensive panels, and
the furniture ornamented with elaborate ivory reliefs (see *BRL*,
cols. 148 f., *IDB* s.v. Ivory, vol. 2, pp. 774 f.). מְהוּמָה 'disorder,
confusion'. The thought is both of the wild life of intoxication
and merrymaking, and of the disintegration of the rule of law, cf.
the following עֲשׁוּקִים 'oppression', 'acts of violence'.

V. 10 is either spoken by the prophet himself (if נאם יהוה is
original) or, less probably, by those who obey the command to
summon the foreign people. נְכֹחָה (fem. of נָכֹחַ*) literally of that
which is straight (e.g. of a road), so of that which is right (cf.
2 Sam. 15.3; Isa. 26.10; 59.14). אָצַר 'gather' (as a store). They do
not gather good things, but heap up injustice by their acts of
violence.

V. 11 introduces the punishment. Instead of reading צַר וּסְבִיב"
'distress (or, enemies) and around the land', it is preferable to
make a slight alteration of the consonantal text by reading י for ו:
צַר יְסֹבֵב" 'distress (or, enemies) will surround the land', cf. the
Syriac version. The subject of הוֹרִד can be the enemies (צַר) or can
be taken as impersonal. The original consonantal text would also
allow the form to be vocalized as a hophal, so that the subject is
עֻזֵּךְ 'your strength', i.e. the fortifications. When the city is captured and laid waste the fortifications will be thrown down into
the valley. נָבוֹז (niphal of בזז) for נָבֹזּוּ (re-formed on the pattern of
the ע"ז verbs, see Gr. § 67t).

V. 12 gives a pictorial description of how Israel will be bat-
tered by disaster. The verse alludes to the law in Exod. 22.12 of
the shepherd's duty to bring the remains of an animal torn by
beasts as evidence that it was a wild animal that had torn it. If he
cannot do this he must pay compensation to the owner (cf. Gen.
31.39; 1 Sam. 17.34 f. and § 266 of the code of Hammurabi).
Amos knows from his experience as a shepherd that the lion only
leaves a couple of leg-bones (כְּרָעַיִם dual) or the meatless lobe of
the ear (בְּדַל אֹזֶן); similarly it will go so hard for Israel when the
enemy comes and tears it apart, that it will only just be possible to
find a couple of insignificant remnants which show that it once
existed. The word 'rescue' has therefore an ironic sound. There

is no more than this in the comparison: the individual details in the image cannot be pressed.

The last part of the verse, which is understood by the Massoretes as attached to בְּנֵי יִשְׂרָאֵל, contains several obscure points, which have caused trouble to the commentators. פֵּאָה means 'edge', 'corner'. But it is a puzzle what can be meant by 'those who sit in Samaria on the edge (or corner) of the couch'. It has been suggested that those who are saved will be so few that they can sit squeezed together on the edge of a bed or couch; but one would expect the expression to be some sort of motivation for the punishment, so that the last line of the verse contains a reproach for their luxurious life. If this is correct it does not help alternatively to connect בִּפְאַת מִטָּה with the verb יִנָּצְלוּ: 'those who live in Samaria will be saved with the corner of the couch', i.e. only with a fragment of the couch, as an expression for how little they save. Several commentators have attempted to remedy the difficulties by embarking on a dubious textual alteration, and reading בְּצִפִּית (for בפאת): 'on the cushion of the couch' (cf. Isa. 21.5). The parallel בִּדְמֶשֶׁק עָרֶשׂ unfortunately does not help with this difficulty, since it is itself problematic. עֶרֶשׂ certainly means 'couch'; but the whole expression cannot mean 'on the silk of the couch', as it is often translated, with the conjecture that דְּמֶשֶׁק is the material damask, named after the city of Damascus. The city's name is written דַּמֶּשֶׂק (note the שׂ, as in 1.3), and apart from this it is most unlikely that the city was already at the time of Amos the home of a well-known textile industry.[1] The LXX thinks of the city of Damascus, but could make nothing of ערשׂ and has transcribed it as ἱερεῖς. BH suggests וּבְעֶרֶשׂ דַּמֶּשֶׂק, but then the parallelism is lost. Others get out of the difficulty by reading דַּבֶּשֶׁת, which is supposed to mean 'cushion' or something similar (cf. the meaning 'camel's hump' in Isa. 30.6). The difficulties in these two uncertain words are of course not avoided if we follow some commentators in linking the line with the following, so that the words become an address in the vocative. The most honest course is to concede that we still have no completely satisfactory interpretation of the passage.

---

[1] Besides, our word 'damask', which is a loan-word from Arabic, has nothing to do with the city Damascus. The Arabic *dimaqs* goes back to metathesis to the Syriac *mitaqs*, which in turn comes from the Greek μέταξα (see S. Fränkel, *Die Aramäischen Fremdwörter im Arabischen*, Leiden 1886, p. 40).

V. 13. Those addressed in the two introductory imperatives can on the traditional division of the verses be either the foreigners addressed in v. 9b, or better the same people to whom the command הַשְׁמִיעוּ in v. 9a is addressed. הָעֵיד בְּ 'solemnly assure', 'enjoin on' (cf. Gen. 43.3).[1] That which they are to enjoin is the content of v. 14 (כִּי = 'that'). The meaning is that they are to warn them in advance of the punishment of Yahweh. בית יעקב means the Northern Kingdom (see on 2.6). The complete expression אדני יהוה אלהי הצבאות 'the Lord Yahweh, the God of hosts' is found in Amos here and in a different order in 5.16. אלהי הצבאות is found again at 6.14, and without the article in 4.13; 5.14, 15, 16, 27; 6.8; further אדני יהוה הצבאות is found in 9.5. It is a disputed question what the hosts in this expression originally were. Some think of the heavenly hosts, including the angels and the stars (see 1 Kgs. 22.19 and Deut. 4.19; Jer. 8.2), others of the armies of Israel, which Yahweh leads (1 Sam. 17.45); others again take the expression as meaning 'the Lord of all powers', so that it is a description of Yahweh as the almighty. All agree that in the course of time the shorter form of the expression יהוה צבאות came to be used as a personal name, the meaning of which was no longer remembered.

V. 14 develops further the content of what they are to enjoin on the house of Jacob. The verb in 14a is construed with the sin in the accusative and the person introduced by עַל, but somewhat differently in 14b, where the altars are the object of the punishment. Bethel (the present Beitin) lay about 17 kilometres north of Jerusalem on the road to Shechem and Samaria. In Bethel and Dan Jeroboam I had set up calves of gold to give the population of the Northern Kingdom a substitute for the temple in Jerusalem (1 Kgs. 12.25 ff.). The sanctuary in Bethel was at the time of Amos one of the most popular in the Northern Kingdom. It was regarded as a royal sanctuary, and came directly under the king (see 7.10, 13; 4.4; 5.5; 9.1; Hos. 4.15; 10.5, 15; 12.5). The city has a prominent place also in the patriarchal narratives, which witness to its significance in ancient Israel (Gen. 12.8; 28.10–22; 35.1–8, cf. also 1 Sam. 10.3). This lasted until the time of Josiah, when he extended his reformation to Bethel, and destroyed the sanctuary there (2 Kgs. 23.15).

---

[1] Others translate 'witness against', so that those addressed are the foreigners of v. 9.

Several recent commentators do not take Bethel here as the city of Bethel but as the god Bethel, so that the reference is to the altars of this god in Samaria, or generally in the whole Northern Kingdom. However, a reference to this god, who is known for instance from the Elephantine texts, and who it has been claimed is found in the Old Testament (e.g. Jer. 48.13), remains less probable here than one to the famous cultic centre, which we do definitely know to have played a part in the story of Amos.[1] Some have found difficulty in the plural מִזְבְּחוֹת, and claim that each sanctuary had only one altar (cf. the following קַרְנוֹת הַמִּזְבֵּחַ). They then correct it to the singular, which does not involve much alteration to the consonantal text. A misreading of מַצֵּבַת 'stone pillar' is not perhaps completely out of the question (see Gen. 28.22). The horns were an important part of the altar (Exod. 27.2; 30.2). The laws of sacrifice prescribe that the blood shall be put on the horns of the altar (Exod. 29.12; Lev. 4.7, 18, 25, 30, 34; Ezek. 43.15, 20), and those who make use of the right of asylum at an altar (see the prescriptions of the law in Exod. 21.12 ff.) cling to its horns (e.g. Adonijah in 1 Kgs. 1.49 ff.; 2.28). When it is said here that the horns of the altar shall be cut off, it is the same as saying that it will completely lose its significance. Altars with projections carved at the corners are known from excavations (see *AOB*, illus. 444 and *ANEP*, 575). It has been conjectured that these 'horns' are really massebas, which symbolize the deity; to make room for the sacrifices they are placed on the four corners of the altar (see *BRL*, s.v. Altar, cols. 13–22, *IDB*, s.v. Altar, vol. I, pp. 96 ff.).

V. 15. The winter house (בֵּית־הַחֹרֶף) must have been built more solidly and with better protection against the cold and rain than the summer house (בֵּית הַקַּיִץ). In the famous scene where King Jehoiakim hears the oracles of Jeremiah read, he sits with a brazier in front of him in the winter house (Jer. 36.22). Some think that the summer house was simply the upper storey which was built on the roof of the house (see Judg. 3.20, where Eglon is sitting here when he receives Ehud), but rich men would certainly have had separate dwellings for the

---

[1] On the god Bethel see O. Eissfeldt, 'Der Gott Bethel', *Archiv für Religionswissenschaft* 28 (1930), pp. 1–30, also in *Kleine Schriften I*, vol. I, Tübingen 1962, pp. 206–33, and J. P. Hyatt, 'The Deity Bethel and the Old Testament', *Journal of the American Oriental Society* 59 (1939), pp. 81–98.

summer.[1] Winter house and summer house are here used collectively. עַל = in addition to. Carvings in ivory were used for the
decoration of the palaces of the rich (שֵׁן literally 'tooth', here
means ivory), cf. 3.9 (and also 6.4; Ps. 45.9 and 1 Kgs. 22.39,
which speaks of King Ahab's house of ivory). Parallel with
the houses of ivory we have בָּתִּים רַבִּים, which is best translated by 'the great houses'. If the parallelism is ignored and the
words translated 'the many houses' (as in Isa. 5.9), it must mean
that the devastation would be thorough. The most attractive
text would be obtained by suggesting a misreading of the rare
word בָּתֵּי הָבְנִים 'houses of ebony' (see Ezek. 27.15), i.e. houses
decorated with ebony.

CHAPTER FOUR

This passage continues from the preceding one. Amos accuses
the women of sharing the guilt in the impoverishment and oppression of the poor, because by their extravagance and luxury
they compel their husbands to provide money for them at the expense of those more poorly placed.

V. 1. The masculine form שִׁמְעוּ is used in place of the feminine.
The women are compared with cows from Bashan, a fertile
country which lies in the land east of the Jordan, east of the territories of Geshur and Maacah, from the river Yarmuk in the south
up to Hermon in the north. It was famous both for its fine oak
forests (Isa. 2.13) and for its fatstock (Deut. 32.14; Ps. 22.13).
While we see something disparaging in comparing the women
with cows, who have nothing else to do but eat fodder until they
are full, oriental writers in fact use the comparison with
thoroughbred cows as a compliment to the women's beauty and
opulence. The point of complaint is that they have led a comfort-
able and luxurious life and made inconsiderate demands on their
husbands, who have only been able to provide the means for this
luxury by injustice to the poor, so that they have in practice paid

---

[1] In the Aramaic inscription of Bar Rekub, l. 19, a summer house is mentioned,
בית כיצא. This inscription is of roughly the same date as Amos (see *NSI*, pp. 180 ff., *KAI*
No. 216).

for the entertainments of the leading women. The verbs עָשַׁק
'oppress' (see 3.9) and רָצַץ 'crush' are used of violations of the
law (cf. 1 Sam. 12.3). לַאדֹנֵיהֶם has the masculine suffix in place of
the feminine suffix. אָדוֹן here means 'husband' (cf. Gen. 18.12).
הָבִיאָה 'bring here' (in the singular, because each says it to her
husband). וְנִשְׁתֶּה can be translated 'so that we can hold parties', as
the corresponding noun מִשְׁתֶּה does not have to be specifically a
drinking party, but can be a party in general. According to Isa.
3.16–4.1 the women in Jerusalem were quite as corrupt as their
sisters in the capital of the Northern Kingdom.

V. 2. For Yahweh to swear by his holiness means that he puts
his divine personality on oath to carry out what he intends (cf.
6.8; 8.7 and Ps. 89.36). The formula 'behold, the days are coming' is often used in eschatological descriptions (see 8.11; 9.13;
1 Sam. 2.31; 2 Kgs. 20.17; Jer. 7.32; 9.24). The phrase is in itself
neutral; only the context shows whether it is a promise or a
threat. Here it is the latter. It is introduced by the consecutive
perfect וְנִשָּׂא, which in form can be either piel or niphal. If it is
taken as a niphal, the following accusative אֶתְכֶם is to be taken as
the object with an impersonal construction in the passive (Gr.
§ 121a–b). In either case we can translate 'they shall take you
up'. As in v. 1 the masculine suffix is used here, but the feminine
suffix subsequently. צִנּוֹת because of the context cannot have the
normal meaning of the word 'shields', but must be taken as a
feminine of צִנִּים 'thorns', and must mean 'hooks', as סִירִים is used
of natural thorns and סִירוֹת of artificial ones, i.e. hooks. דּוּגָה must
mean 'fishing' (hapax legomenon); סִירוֹת דּוּגָה therefore means
fishing-hooks. The LXX on the other hand has taken סִיר in the
sense of 'cooking pot', but has not given a rendering of the word
דּוּגָה. The image used illustrates how they were to be carried away
like fish which are suddenly plucked up out of the water. The
deportation happens to them all, even if in the first instance some
are left over (cf. 'what remains of you'). For the image used here
cf. Hab. 1.14 f.; Jer. 16.16; Ezek. 29.4. The suggestion has been
made that the two expressions אתכם and אחריתכן should correspond to one another and that אתכם should be corrected to אַפְּכֶן
'your nose', so that the women are compared with the corpses of
animals which are dragged away with a hook in the nose and in
the back אָחֹר = אַחֲרִית). By this a continuation of the image of v. 1
is obtained. But this understanding of the passage does not fit

with the word דּוּגָה, which points to a change in the image. The
MT should therefore be retained.

V. 3. The enemy will storm and capture the city, so that the
women will have to leave as prisoners through the breaches that
have been made in the wall (פְּרָצִים is accusative, see Gr.
§ 118d ff.). תצאנה could alternatively be vocalized as a hophal
תֻּצֶאנָה: 'you shall be taken out' (cf. LXX). אִשָּׁה נֶגְדָּה 'each one
straight ahead', i.e. they must go straight ahead without turning
aside in any direction, and keep strictly to their position in the
line of prisoners. For נֶגֶד with reflexive suffix in the sense of
'straight ahead' cf. Josh. 6.5, 20. Perhaps the phrase can also be
translated 'one by one', i.e. they must go in a row like cows,
which go one by one through an opening in the fence. The following two words are a crux interpretum. וְהִשְׁלַכְתֶּנָה 'you will
throw' (with the irregular ending תֶּנָה־ for תֵּן־, if ה is not the
result of dittography) cannot have the following הַהַרְמוֹנָה as its
object, since this is formed with the hē locale (note the accentua-
tion). The easiest solution would be to alter the vocalization of
the verbal form to the hophal הָשְׁלַכְתֶּנָה: 'you will be thrown' (cf.
LXX) and understand the following word as the place where
they will be taken to in captivity. Some of the ancient translations
understand the following word as Armenia; it would in that case
have to be vocalized הַר מִנִּי 'the mountain(s) of Minni' (cf. Jer.
51.27, where Minni corresponds to Mannai in the Assyrian cuneiform texts, and means a part of Armenia, cf. BDB). Others make
a slight correction to חֶרְמוֹנָה 'to Hermon', the well-known
mountain north of Bashan, and think that the cows are to go back
to where they belong (see on v. 1), or that this only signifies the
direction in which they are to be carried away, so that it is a circumlocution for deportation to Assyria (cf. 5.27: 'I will take you
beyond Damascus'). Apart from these suggestions there are
numerous other conjectures, which are clear evidence of the ingenuity of the commentators, but contain no guarantee that they
are correct.

Vv. 4–5: An ironical demand to the people to continue with the corrupt cult

V. 4. In the rest of the chapter Amos no longer speaks to the
women alone, but to the whole people (cf. 'O people of Israel' in

v. 5). The following demands to practise the cult in the correct manner are intended ironically, as appears clearly from the words וּפִשְׁעוּ 'and sin!', by which judgement is passed on their cult. It is possible that Amos begins by imitating the style of the pilgrimage song to catch the attention of his hearers. The people were of the view that the festivals were pleasing to Yahweh. They thought that the cult followed from the covenant with Yahweh, and that sacrifice was a means to keep the blessings or to secure them anew, if they had for any reason angered Yahweh. On the other hand they regard it as out of the question that Yahweh could annul the covenant and forsake the people. The prophets as a whole, not only Amos, protested strongly against this understanding of the cult, asserting that Yahweh takes no pleasure at all in sacrifices, and has not demanded them. Instead they enjoin the ethical demands of love of one's neighbour which follow from the covenant with Yahweh. Only by keeping these commandments can the people escape the punishment, which may even involve the end of the people, if they do not repent in time. How far the prophets rejected the cult completely, or only the degenerate cult which assigned to sacrifices an overriding significance at the expense of the ethical commandments, is an old problem which we will return to in connection with chapter 5. For Bethel see on 3.14. Gilgal (literally 'stone circle', so with the article, Gr. § 125e) was the first place where the people pitched camp after the crossing of the Jordan, not far from Jericho (Josh. 4.19 f.). The importance of the city as a cultic centre is shown by its frequent mention (5.5; Hos. 4.15; 9.15; 12.12; 1 Sam. 7.16; 11.14 and many other passages). In the earliest period it was probably the sacral centre of the confederation of the Joseph tribes. It was earlier held that there was another Gilgal in the neighbourhood of Bethel, where Elisha dwelt (2 Kgs. 2.1; 4.38), but it is now the general view that there was only one Gilgal, near Jericho. Archaeologists think they can point to it in Chirbet el Mefjir, two kilometres north of Jericho (see *BRL*, cols. 197 f., and (as 'probable') *IDB*, vol. 2, p. 398). Before הַגִּלְגָּל it is usual to understand בֹּאוּ from the beginning of the verse and to insert an 'and' before הַרְבּוּ. The text can, however, be translated: 'sin much in Gilgal'. הַרְבּוּ serves as an auxiliary verb with the main verb introduced by the infinitive construct with לְ (Gr. § 120 ff.). The following line should not as some have suggested be translated: 'bring your sacrifices every morning and your tithes every third day', so that it becomes an ironical demand to go beyond the normal practice, according to which each brought his sacrifice once a year (see 1 Sam. 1.3, 7, 21) and his tithe payments every third year.[1] A sacrifice every day (? distributive) and tithe payment every third day is too improbable an exaggeration. Rather the passage points to an otherwise unattested custom that people brought their sacrifice the day after their arrival and their tithe payments on the third day (i.e. two days after arrival). The prophet sarcastically demands of them that they should observe these rules exactly. זֶבַח is the blood sacrifice, with which is connected a sacrificial feast, the same as שֶׁלֶם 'feast sacrifice'. At harvest time it was the custom of the Hebrews as of other ancient peoples to pay a certain share of the harvest to the sanctuary with which people were connected. The thought underlying this is not only that God should have a share as a gift, but originally quite as much that the crop should be sanctified by the god getting his share, so that the people themselves are able to enjoy the rest. It is the same principle that we meet in the laws about the firstfruits, with the difference that there the quantities play a subordinate part; it is for example sufficient to bring a single sheaf of wheat. With tithe on the other hand the amount to be paid is fixed at this quite definite proportion. In the book of the covenant (Exod. 21–23) there is no prescription about tithes, but Deuteronomy contains detailed rules about them (12.6 f., 17 f.; 14.22 ff.; 26.12 ff.). Formally they concern the sanctuary in Jerusalem and forbid payments to all others, but in reality they give us an insight into how men with their families came to shrines all over the land to make their payments of tithes, and held a feast together with the priests (see J. Pedersen, *Israel*, vols. III–IV, London and Copenhagen 1940, pp. 307 ff.). The narrative in Gen. 28.10–22 seeks to establish the right of the sanctuary at Bethel to the tithe from the promise that the patriarch Jacob made after Yahweh's appearance to him.

V. 5. The introductory infinitive absolute קַטֵּר has the same

---

[1] This point rests upon a false interpretation of Deut. 14.28 and 26.12. Tithes were certainly brought every year, but every third year they were to be given to Levites, to the sojourner, the fatherless and the widow (see 14.29). In consequence there is no possibility of producing a satisfactory sense by translating יָמִים by 'year', as in 1 Sam. 1.21, and elsewhere.

meaning as the surrounding imperatives (Gr. § 113bb); it is therefore not necessary to alter the vocalization to קַטֵּר. The verb in the piel (and in the hiphil) means to let (an offering) go up as smell or smoke (cf. קְטֹרֶת (1) 'the smell of sacrifice' (2) 'incense'). תּוֹדָה 'a sacrifice of praise' or 'a thank-offering' is, as appears from the name, a sacrifice that is offered in thankfulness for one reason or another. Lev. 7.11 f. prescribes that if one brings a peace offering as a thanksgiving, one should offer apart from the sacrificial animal unleavened cakes, etc. This is corroborated by the prohibition of leaven in Lev. 2.11, cf. Exod. 23.18. On the other hand Lev. 7.13 and 23.17 speak of leavened bread. The passage in Amos shows that at this time the use of leavened bread[1] in connection with the sacrificial animal was regarded as the best manner of making a sacrifice. Roughly prepared unleavened bread is of course older than leavened bread, and had therefore probably survived for a long time in the cult. At the time of Amos, however, the new and more refined custom of using leavened bread had gained admittance to the cult. The contradictory provisions in the laws come therefore from different times. נְדָבָה 'free will offering' is an offering which is brought as an expression of an inner urge, and not from distress or other similar cause. It is listed together with other sacrifices in the laws (Lev. 7.16; 22.18; Deut. 12.16, 17, etc.).

The eagerness of the people to proclaim their good deeds reminds us of the behaviour which Jesus condemns in Matt. 6.2. This form of service is something which the Israelites took delight in, but Amos makes them aware that it is not according to Yahweh's will and that it will not prevent him from punishing them.

Vv. 6–11: Yahweh has tried in vain with five punishments to show the people that they are on the wrong track

The description of each of the punishments ends with the refrain: 'and yet you did not return to me'. The context demands that the verbal forms in this passage should be rendered in English by a past tense. In another context the consecutive perfect

---

[1] מֵחָמֵץ must mean 'of leavened bread', not privatively 'without unleavened bread'.

וְהִמְטַרְתִּי in v. 7 and the imperfects would be rendered by a future. It should be remembered that originally at least the Hebrew verbs are not tenses but aspects.

V. 6. וְגַם 'and yet' is connected with the whole clause, not just with אֲנִי. The connection with the preceding passage can be roughly paraphrased as follows: otherwise you would have had to realize that your cult is not pleasing to me, since I have time and again attempted to bring you to repentance by the plagues that I sent upon you. The first of the plagues consisted in a famine across the whole land. נִקְיוֹן שִׁנַּיִם literally 'cleanness of teeth', i.e. the teeth had nothing to chew on. Instead of נִקְיוֹן several of the old translations read קִהְיוֹן 'bluntness'. But the parallel expression 'lack of bread' is an argument for the MT. שׁוּב עַד is stronger than שׁוּב אֶל, since עַד signifies that the movement reaches its mark completely, but אֶל only means 'towards'. The Christian use of the expression 'to turn again' in the sense of 'repent' has its origin in the frequent Old Testament use of שׁוּב in a religious sense (see Isa. 10.21; 21.6; 55.7; Hos. 6.1; 14.2; Deut. 4.30).

V. 7. The second plague was a disastrous drought. In Palestine the year can roughly be divided into a dry season and a rainy season. In the latter half of October the rain begins to fall again after the dry period, when everything is parched, and the ground hard and unsuitable for the sowing of corn. This rain, which marks the beginning of the rainy season and lasts until the beginning of December, is called 'the former rain' יוֹרֶה (or מוֹרֶה, Joel 2.23).

After this the rain falls at intervals through the winter until the end of February. The wells and streams are filled by the winter rain. Then in the spring, in March and April, there are heavy showers again, the so-called 'latter rain' מַלְקוֹשׁ, which determines the final growth and ripening of the corn. The corn-harvest (קָצִיר) takes place at the end of April and in May. The word גֶּשֶׁם can be used of heavy rain (Gen. 7.12) in contrast to the general word for rain מָטָר; it can also comprise both the former and the latter rain (Joel 2.23) or be used of the whole rainy or winter season (Cant. 2.11, cf. in the plural Ezra 10.9, 13). The thought here is no doubt not that Yahweh holds back the former rain until there are only three months to harvest, but that the winter rain has stopped too soon, and the latter rain failed. That meant that the cisterns stood empty, and the corn suffered serious loss,

with a much reduced harvest in consequence. מָנַע 'hold back'.
בְּעוֹד שְׁלֹשָׁה״ = 'when there were still three months to harvest'.
It is characteristic of the rain in Palestine that it falls in heavy
showers and very unevenly, so that different regions have very
varied amounts. חֶלְקָה 'portion', 'piece of ground'. תַּמְטִיר must be
understood impersonally ('which it did not rain on'); the LXX
read the first person.

V. 8. Worn out by thirst, the population of a couple of cities
staggered around to find water elsewhere, because the water in
their own wells and cisterns had dried up as a consequence of the
drought, but they were disappointed in the place they came to.
נוע is not 'to wander around' (as in Gen. 4.12 and Amos 8.12), but
'to stagger around' (of exhaustion). For the sequence of numbers
two—three cf. the expression three—four in chapters 1–2. שבע is
not here used of being filled but of quenching one's thirst.

V. 9. The third plague is given as the parching of the corn
(שְׁדָּפוֹן, cf. Gen. 41.6). When the hot desert wind (the 'sirocco')
blows, the grass and the corn wither. In place of their natural
green they both acquire a sickly yellow colour; this is the allusion
in יֵרָקוֹן, which is related to the root ירק 'to be yellow-green'. The
word therefore properly means 'becoming yellow', i.e. 'withering'. The RSV renders the two words by 'blight' and 'mildew'.
The same two words are found together in Deut. 28.22; 1 Kgs.
8.37; Hagg. 2.17. The trouble was made worse by a plague of
locusts, which devastated the orchards and vineyards. Although
the MT gives a possible meaning, 'in quantity (הַרְבּוֹת) the locust
laid waste your gardens', most prefer to correct הַרְבּוֹת to הֶחֱרַבְתִּי
'I dried up'. Wine, figs and olives are the most important products of the land after corn. The devastation of the olive-trees in
particular is felt in many spheres, because olive oil is used as a
food, a cosmetic and a medicament (Luke 10.34), and is used as a
fuel in lamps (Matt. 25.1 ff.). תְּאֵנָה, plural תְּאֵנִים (1) 'fig-tree' (as
here) (2) 'the fig'. גָּזָם 'locust' (from גָּזַם 'to cut off'); the name
'the gnawer' alludes to the fact that the locust gnaws everything
away. In Joel's description of a plague of locusts four completely
different words for locust are used (see Driver's excursus on
locusts in his commentary on Joel and Amos, ed. 2, pp. 84–93).[1]

---

[1] On the devastations caused by swarms of locusts see L. Schneller, *Kennst du das Land?*,
Jerusalem 1888, rev. ed. Leipzig 1894, pp. 136 ff., and further G. Dalman, *Arbeit und Sitte
in Palästina* I, Gütersloh 1928, pp. 393–5, and II, Gütersloh 1932, pp. 344–8.

V. 10. For the fourth plague they were afflicted with pestilence (דֶּבֶר) and war. בְּדֶרֶךְ מִצְרַיִם 'in the manner of Egypt' is according to some an allusion to the fact that plague as such was one of the ten plagues of Egypt (Exod. 5.3), according to others that Egypt in general was notorious for its unhealthy climate, and therefore often afflicted with infectious illness (Deut. 7.15; 28.60). Either interpretation is possible. On the other hand בְּדֶרֶךְ מִצְרַיִם should not be translated 'on the way to Egypt', since the wars which are alluded to in the next phrase are probably the wars against Syria in the time before the activity of Amos, so that the plague which arose in connection with the wars is compared with the notorious plague of Egypt. It is of course of no great significance that plague is mentioned first, since war and plague belong closely together in the consciousness of the ancients.[1] In the wars against Syria Israel suffered severe losses both of men and of horses (see 2 Kgs. 13.7). עִם שְׁבִי סוּסֵיכֶם literally: 'together with the taking captive of your horses' = 'apart from the fact that your horses were taken captive'. The corpses of the young men that had been slain piled up and lay unburied, so that they fouled the air with their smell (cf. Isa. 34.3). וּבְאַפְּכֶם 'and in your nose', i.e. up into your nose. Many delete the ו as superfluous.

V. 11. The last and worst plague was an earthquake, which is compared with the destruction of the two cities of Sodom and Gomorrah (Gen. 19.24 f.). כְּמַהְפֵּכַת אֱלֹהִים has the sound of a proverbial phrase. It is the expression that is always used when the destruction of the two cities is mentioned (Isa. 13.19; Jer. 49.18; 50.40; Deut. 29.22). מַהְפֵּכָה is related to the verb הָפַךְ 'overthrow' (with בְּ: 'at, among'), which is also used in the description of the destruction of Sodom and Gomorrah (Gen. 19.21, 25, 29).[2] This is described in Genesis 19 as somewhat like an earthquake, accompanied by a volcanic eruption with a hail of sulphur and of fire. It can be ascribed to dependence on this narrative that Amos subsequently compares the people with a brand (אוּד, cf. Isa. 7.4) which is saved from the fire. The image does not necessarily indicate more than how hard pressed the people were (cf.

---

[1] According to the Assyrian eponym lists plague was prevalent in the years 803, 765 and 759 B.C. (see E. Schrader, *Die Keilinschriften und das Alte Testament*, ed. 3 rev. H. Zimmern and H. Winckler, Berlin 1903, pp. 481–5).

[2] מהפכת must be regarded as a verbal noun which like the infinitive construct can both stand in the construct state and govern a following object (cf. Gen. 2.4), see Gr. § 115d.

Zech. 3.2). Some have thought that the disaster was in fact accompanied by conflagration. This is indeed not out of the question, since fire from the hearths can easily set fire to houses when they are suddenly overturned. The earthquake which is alluded to cannot of course be the same one that is mentioned in the heading 1.1, since that occurred two years after the appearance of Amos, while 4.11 speaks of an earthquake in the past. Since earthquakes are quite frequent in Palestine, it should not surprise us that this one is not mentioned in the Old Testament. The one which is alluded to in 1.1 must have been more violent still.

V. 12 introduces the judgement with לָכֵן (see on 3.11). It is not said in what the punishment consists. All that is said is: 'I will do thus (כֹּה) with you, O Israel'. Some have supposed that the punishment has been omitted because it offended a later copyist, and has been replaced with the imprecise כֹּה. One should rather think of the words as accompanied by a threatening gesture, which left the listeners in no doubt of the serious nature of the punishment. The following זֹאת refers to the punishment that has been alluded to. The people are urged to prepare to meet their god (cf. 9.15), who does not come to save, as people had expected, but to judge. For לִקְרַאת 'to meet' from קרא = קרה see Gr. § 74h.

V. 13. The concluding doxology which describes the might of Yahweh serves to assure the hearers that he will also be able to carry out what he threatens. It is therefore a complete misunderstanding that many commentators have wanted to explain both this doxology and the two in 5.8 f. and 9.5 f. as secondary because they do not fit the style of the context. Of the two verbs which describe Yahweh's creative power, the first belongs properly with the picture of the potter (יוֹצֵר) who forms his vessel of clay (Isa. 45.9), but is used also of God's capacity to form living beings of dead material (Gen. 2.7, 8, 19). The other verb בָּרָא is used in the Old Testament in the sense of 'create' only with God as subject (Gen. 1.1; Isa. 40.28; 42.5; 45.18; Ps. 51.12, etc.). Even if the ancient Hebrews did not grapple with the abstract idea which in dogmatic theology is called 'creatio ex nihilo', they felt that this verb expressed God's sovereign power to create what he wanted, without a pattern in anything already existing (see the commentaries on Gen. 1.1). The two verbs, which are used here without any serious difference, are found in parallel also in Isa. 43.1, 7 and 45.18. Yahweh's creation of the mountains and the wind (רוּחַ,

here hardly in the sense of 'the spirit') are mentioned as two especially conspicuous wonders in nature. The conclusion of the line expresses his wisdom. שֵׂחַ* (only here) no doubt means 'thought', 'consideration', the same word as שִׂיחַ (Ps. 55.3; 104.34; Job 7.13; 1 Sam. 1.16 and other passages). The suffix in שֵׂחוֹ is best taken in context as referring to אָדָם, not to Yahweh (if the latter were the case, it would be a parallel to 3.7). It can be mentioned as a curiosity of criticism that some commentators have wanted to understand אדם as a personal name and seen an allusion in the passage to Gen. 3.11. The expression can be compared to Jer. 11.20: 'Yahweh tests the kidneys and the heart'. The next expression עֹשֵׂה שַׁחַר עֵיפָה refers again to his might in nature. The MT must be translated 'he who makes the dawn darkness', i.e. can suddenly darken the bright dawn with dark stormclouds (cf. in part Isa. 50.3; on the other hand the reference in 5.8b is to the regular course of day and night). The LXX read 'and' between the two words: 'he who makes the dawn and darkness'. The following 'he who strides over the heights of the earth' is also to be taken as an expression of his might. He shows his lordship over the highest places of the earth by moving over them, cf. Mic. 1.3 and Job 9.8 ('he strides over the wavetops of the sea'). In the form בָּמֳתֵי the masculine ending ē of the construct state is added to the feminine ending -ōt. The Massoretes have vocalized the word as if it came from בֹּמֶת, not from בָּמָה (see Gr. §87s). The name of Yahweh stands last for emphasis (see on 3.13), as it also does in 5.27 to give emphasis to the preceding utterance (cf. Isa. 47.4; 48.2; 51.15; Jer. 31.35, etc.).

CHAPTER FIVE

Vv. 1–3: A lament over Israel

V. 1. The prophet raises a lament over the people. He imitates a funeral lament both in expression and in rhythm (the so-called *qina* rhythm, which shows a basic pattern of 3 + 2 stressed syllables). At the bier of the departed gathered the professional mourners (Jer. 9.16), in the New Testament period also fluteplayers (Matt. 9.23), or the relations and friends of the departed

(2 Sam. 1.17), and began the lamentation. In the poetic usage of the Old Testament the individual lament is also transferred to the death of a collective unit, i.e. the fall of a city, a tribe or a people. Amos is the first writer with whom such a 'political' lament is found (cf. later Isa. 14.4–21; Ezek. 27.2–10). We can picture him appearing during the feast at Bethel and suddenly tearing the participants away from their revelry by starting the mournful tones of the lament, so that when they listen to him, they are seized with terror and perhaps also with indignation to hear that it is the death of Israel that he is lamenting. נָשָׂא 'lift up' = 'sound' (cf. נָשָׂא קוֹל 'raise one's voice'). The content of the lament follows in v. 2. קִינָה can either be understood as a second accusative with the verb נָשָׂא ('the word which I raise as a lament') or in apposition to הַדָּבָר ('the word which I raise, a lament'). בית ישראל = the Northern Kingdom.

V. 2. In the lament itself the prophet uses the perfects נָפְלָה and נִטְּשָׁה because the people are thought of as already fallen and cast down. Each of the two perfects has attached to it a circumstantial clause, which signifies the helplessness of the people. In the proper Semitic manner the nation is personified in the poem as a woman. This is a representation which fits well with the fact that cities and lands are feminine in Hebrew. The fact that it is a virgin does not indicate that this is the first time Israel has been defeated, nor does it increase the sorrow over her early death, but is a feature related to the representation of Israel as a beautiful young woman. The construct relationship בתולת ישראל is in sense the same as 'the virgin Israel' (Gr. § 128k). נִטְּשָׁה (niphal of נָטַשׁ) is usually translated by 'be cast down' because the basic meaning in the qal seems to be 'cast down' or 'abandon'. It is possible that the niphal here signifies 'be forsaken' (cf. the pual in Isa. 32.14), which fits the following clause. The painfulness of her position is increased by the fact that it happens on her own land.

V. 3. While v. 2 is given as the prophet's own words, the basis for the lament follows here in the form of an utterance of Yahweh, which predicts that only a tenth shall escape disaster. The survival of a remnant corresponds to the passages in the book which do not look to a total destruction of the people, but encourage hope of a happier future later (see on 9.11 ff.); in this context, however, the saying is to be understood primarily as a threat. הַיֹּצֵאת אֶלֶף 'who marches out as a thousand' or 'with a thousand' (for the accusative see Gr. § 117z). The passage presupposes a military system in which it is the cities, not as in the earliest times families and tribes, which provide men for war. Certainly very few cities will have been in a position to provide a contingent of a thousand men, but the numbers are primarily to be understood as illustrations of the imminent decimation of the people. 2 Sam. 18.1 has the same division into units of a thousand and a hundred, which are led respectively by commanders of thousands and commanders of hundreds; 1 Sam. 8.12 has in addition the smaller unit of fifty men. תַּשְׁאִיר = 'have left over'.

Vv. 4–6: A demand to seek Yahweh himself and not the cultic centres

V. 4. If כִּי is taken in the sense of 'for', the verse is understood as giving the reasons for the preceding warning of disaster. Then the sense is that Israel is going to suffer the punishment that has been announced if it disregards the warnings of Yahweh (cf. below). The effect of this connection, however, is rather artificial, and כִּי is better taken as a particle effecting a transition between the two passages, which are loosely connected to one another: 'but' or 'yet'. דָּרַשׁ is often used as a technical expression for turning to a sanctuary to learn God's will in one matter or another through an oracle (Gen. 25.22; 1 Sam. 9.9; 2 Kgs. 3.11; 8.8). Here Amos uses the word in a peculiar way. He first condemns the people for turning to the three much frequented pilgrimage centres which were connected with the Yahweh cult, but then demands that they should seek Yahweh. The first form of 'seeking' was objectionable because visits to a sanctuary only led to feasts and debauchery; when the people had brought their offerings and taken part in the feasts they thought that they had done all that the covenant with Yahweh prescribed, and did not take into consideration any duty to observe the ethical commandments. For this reason the prophet declaims against these cultic centres, even though they were dedicated to Yahweh and were connected with the earliest history of the nation. In contrast to this he makes the demand to seek Yahweh, which must be understood as meaning to seek out and observe his commandments, which stress not offerings but a moral way of life (cf. on 4.5). To seek Yahweh means roughly the same therefore as what v. 14 calls 'to seek the good'. Only such seeking will help them through the danger that threatens. To seek Yahweh does not on the other hand mean, as some have suggested, to turn to the temple in Jerusalem where Yahweh has his proper dwelling-place (1.2). Amos would then be a sort of forerunner of Deuteronomy with its insistence on the one correct dwelling-place. Amos' polemic against the cult of his time was not, however, something in which he was alone. Somewhat later Isaiah too declaimed against the cult in Jerusalem. This is reason enough to suggest that the problem in Amos does not turn on seeking the only correct sanctuary. One would also have to expect other definitely positive declarations in Amos of the significance of Jerusalem, if this interpretation of 'seeking Yahweh' were correct. The 'seeking' that Amos commended to the people was to help them through the threatening danger. The two imperatives דִּרְשׁוּנִי וִחְיוּ are related to one another as condition and consequence (Gr. § 110f). By חיה is meant not eternal life but survival of the impending danger of death which confronts the people if they do not repent in time. Here Amos counts on the possibility that the people can and perhaps will reform. At other times the picture seems to have looked darker to him (e.g. 5.27), unless one should in fact understand his words of judgement as conditional threats (see further on this problem on 9.8 ff.).

V. 5. On Bethel and Gilgal see on 3.14 and 4.4. The third sanctuary mentioned is בְּאֵר שֶׁבַע, which was not in the Northern Kingdom, but in the extreme south of Judah (cf. the phrase 'the whole of Israel from Dan to Beersheba', 1 Sam. 3.20, as a description of Israel from north to south). For this reason they had to 'cross the frontier' (עָבַר) if they went on pilgrimage there from the Northern Kingdom. In popular belief it was connected with well-known occasions in the lives of the patriarchs (Gen. 21.22–33; 22.19; 26.23–25, 31–33; 28.10; 46.1). How highly the people regarded this sanctuary is shown by the fact that the population of the Northern Kingdom still went on pilgrimage to it in the time of Amos.[1] With a word-play which cannot be rendered in

---

[1] According to Alt there was a sanctuary here for 'the Fear of Isaac' already before the time of the conquest, where he was worshipped by a wider circle than just the neighbouring tribes (see A. Alt, *Der Gott der Väter* (BWANT series III, vol. 12), Stuttgart 1929, pp. 57 f. = *Kleine Schriften zur Geschichte des Volkes Israel* I, Munich 1953, p. 53, ET *Essays on Old Testament History and Religion*, Oxford 1966, p. 52).

English the fall of Gilgal is threatened.[1] Deportation (גָּלֹה 'go
into exile') of the population of a conquered land or of part of it
was a method which the Assyrians employed to keep their subject
peoples under control. The name of Bethel is taken as the starting-
point for the punishment which will befall the city, the last part
of the city's name being altered from אֵל 'God' to אָוֶן, which is an
expression for the powers of evil, but also for that which is empty
and powerless, which has no existence in itself (Isa. 41.29). In the
Psalms פֹּעֲלֵי אָוֶן can be rendered by 'those who practise wizardry'
or 'magic'. Mowinckel[2] translates the passage here very appropriately: 'Bethel becomes a house of ogres', alluding to the idea
that ogres and demons dwell in the ruins of devastated cities
(Isa. 13.21; 34.12, 14). Hosea has the same corruption of the
name of Bethel, simply calling it Beth-awen (Hos. 4.15; 5.8;
10.5, cf. also Josh. 7.2; 18.12; 1 Sam. 13.5; 14.23). No threat is
directed against Beersheba.

V. 6. The demand of v. 4 to seek Yahweh is repeated, but
accompanied by a new warning. צָלַח means 'to press in on'; it is
used (with עַל or אֶל) of the spirit when it comes over a man (of
Samson Judg. 14.6, of Saul 1 Sam. 10.6 and of David 1 Sam.
16.13). With the accusative it can be used for 'to press forward'
to a place (2 Sam. 19.18). We can take Yahweh as the subject of
the verb and translate: 'so that he may not press forward to the
house of Joseph as a fire'. Others would translate צָלַח by 'set fire
to'; the translation fits the context and finds support in Sir. 8.10,
where the verb has this meaning (cf. also the LXX: ἀναλάμψῃ).
It is therefore unnecessary to make an alteration of the text (as
BH) to produce this meaning or to obtain reasonable sense. The
house of Joseph is the Northern Kingdom, of which the most important tribes were the Joseph tribes. With וְאָכְלָה the subject is
אֵשׁ, which is feminine. As the parallel to the house of Joseph the
LXX reads בֵּית ישׂראל. MT's בֵּית־אֵל is not impossible. Bethel is
stressed as the place that Yahweh's anger is especially directed
against, so that he allows it to burn down, without anyone inter-
vening to fight the fire.

---

[1] Wellhausen (p. 5) produces a word-play in German: 'Gilgal wird zum Galgen gehn
und Bethel wird des Teufels werden' (Gilgal will go to the gallows, and Bethel will become the devil's). Similar plays on words with the names of cities are found in Isa. 10.30;
Hos. 12.12; Mic. 1.10–14.

[2] *Det gamle Testamente oversatt*, S. Michelet, S. Mowinckel, N. Messel, III De senere
profeter, Oslo 1944 (on Amos 5.5).

V. 7 contains a mention of those who corrupt justice. The verse seems so strange in context that it is not surprising that many attempts have been made to find the right explanation of it. Some would understand the participle with the article as a vocative, so that the demand in the preceding verse is directed to those who corrupt justice. It cannot, however, be denied that such a vocative would drag heavily behind the sentence. Nor does it fit well in apposition to 'the house of Joseph' or to 'Bethel'. Others assume therefore that the article has arisen from a misunderstood הוֹי 'Woe to' (cf. 5.18; 6.1). The verse in this case becomes a cry of lament. But this has a poor connection with the preceding verse and hardly any with the verse immediately following. To remedy this some commentators assume that there has been a dislocation of the original order of the verses, and that vv. 8–9 should really follow after v. 10 (cf. *BH*), or v. 7 after v. 9. This sort of mistake is not inconceivable. A copyist may have forgotten a verse, and afterwards when he discovered this added it in the margin or at the foot of the column. In a later copy the verse may have been inserted again into the text, but at the wrong place. This last solution undoubtedly produces the most intelligible text, but that is not to say that it is also the original one. הפך with לְ = 'to change something into'. לַעֲנָה is a bitter plant; we can appropriately translate it 'wormwood' (it is certainly one of the different sorts of artemisia which are found in Palestine). Bitterness is a natural metaphor for harmfulness, so that the prophet means by this image that justice instead of bringing well-being to the whole community has poisoned it (cf. 6.12). The reproach by its contents reminds us of 2.6–8 and 4.1. 'Cast down righteousness to the earth' is the opposite of to 'set it on its feet' (הִצִּיג) in v. 15. The expression is originally based on treating justice as a living being, but it is subsequently used in a transferred sense.

Vv. 8–9: A description of Yahweh's might

V. 8. The introductory participle is not appropriate as a continuation of v. 7, but follows on without difficulty after the word יהוה in v. 6, so that the description of Yahweh's might gives the preceding warning increased seriousness, like the concluding doxology in 4.13. כִּימָה (only here and Job 9.9; 38.31) is the name of a constellation or of an individual star. Most commentators suppose that it is the Pleiades, but some that it is the bright star Sirius. כְּסִיל is certainly the constellation Orion (cf. Job. 9.9; 38.31; in the plural the word is used of the constellations in general, Isa. 13.10). The name means 'fool' and allows us to conjecture that a piece of mythology or a legend unknown to us lies behind it.[1] The creation of these two well-known constellations is a testimony to Yahweh's wonderful might. The next two expressions adduce the regular change between day and night as evidence of Yahweh's power. The massoretic vocalization of צַלְמָוֶת interprets the word as 'shadow of death' (composed of צֵל and מָוֶת), and this is how the LXX has understood the word too; on the other hand the objection can be made that shade in general is not regarded as an evil by people in the Near East, and although the apposition of the word death could make the shadow something sinister, it is preferable to connect the word with the root צלם 'be dark' as a noun with the ending -ūt, or perhaps better the plural ending -ōt. The word then signifies the deepest darkness (intensive plural). This gives a good correspondence to the word morning here. The words together are parallel to the following expression, day and night. החשׁיך is constructed with two accusatives ('darkens day to night'). 'He who calls on the waves of the sea and pours them out upon the earth' (cf. 9.6) can be taken either as a single occasion (as at the beginning of the verse) i.e. a violent inundation, perhaps referring to the flood of Genesis, or as something that Yahweh does continuously (cf. the allusion to the change from day to night). In the latter case the thought is of the cycle of water going from sea to sky and back again (Job 36.27 ff. and perhaps Isa. 55.10). The waters must obey Yahweh's voice when he calls (see Job 38.34). For the conclusion 'Yahweh is his name' cf. 4.13 and 9.6.

V. 9 expresses Yahweh's might in the world of men, where he punishes the great powers when they evoke his disapproval. The basic meaning of בלג is, as Arabic shows, 'shine' or 'be glad'; the hiphil therefore means either transitively 'let shine' (as here) or intransitively 'be glad' (Ps. 39.14; Job 9.27; 10.20 f.). If Yahweh lets devastation shine or flash out over fortresses (עַז the pausal form of עוֹז 'might', 'fortress', see 3.11), this in effect means their

---

[1] On the stars in the Old Testament see S. Mowinckel, *Die Sternnamen im Alten Testament*, Supplement to *NTT* 29 (1928).

sudden fall. מִבְצָר is another word for fortress. 9b is a consecutive clause, which is dependent on 9a.[1]

Vv. 10–13: Against lawlessness and greed among the rich

V. 10 joins naturally on to v. 7, which introduces a condemnation of the injustice which is rampant among the people. By 'the gate' is meant the city gate, where public legal hearings took place. The city wall was as a rule strengthened and widened at the place where the gate was, so that a large space was formed. Here court sittings were held, presided over by the elders of the city (Deut. 21.19 f.; 22.15 ff.; 25.7 ff.; Ruth 4.1 ff.). Before the city gate (i.e. inside it)[2] there was sometimes an open space, where large meetings were held (Neh. 8.1, cf. 2 Chron. 32.6). At the gate, too, men met and conducted business (2 Kgs. 7.1). 'The gate' is therefore equivalent to 'the court' or 'the market'(cf. Latin *forum*).[3]

The hiphil of יכח can mean 'to supervise litigation', 'to judge' (Gen. 31.42; Isa. 11.3); in that case מוֹכִיחַ must be understood as referring to the judge. But the verb can also mean 'to conduct a case' (אֶל 'against', Job 13.3). In that case the מוֹכִיחַ here is the one who presents the case of the poor before the court. The parallel דֹּבֵר תָּמִים can if necessary be understood as referring to the judge who gives his verdict honestly, but better of all who speak out

---

[1] *BH* (following G. Hoffmann, 'Versuche zu Amos', *ZAW* 3 (1883), pp. 110 f.) corrects the text so that the content corresponds to v. 8a. שׁד is corrected to שׁר 'Taurus' (the bull), עַשׁ is read עֵז 'Capella' (the goat), and מבצר is vocalized מְבַצֵּר 'Vindemiator', the grape gatherer, a star in the constellation Virgo. The translation is then: 'he who causes Taurus and Capella to rise, and causes Taurus and Vindemiator to set' (hiphil וְהֵבִיא). To make sense of the verse it makes the further assumption that it stood originally before v. 8.

[2] In Tell en-Nasbeh, however, there has also been found an example of an area with long stone benches outside the gate; see C. C. McCown, *Tell en-Nasbeh I*, Berkeley and New Haven 1947, p. 196.

[3] Archaeological discoveries do not in general seem to allow the possibility of places of assembly anywhere else than at the city gate (as against Mowinckel's article 'I porten' in the Buhl Festschrift (*Studier tilegnede Prof. Dr. Phil. & Theol. Frants Buhl*, ed. J. Jacobsen, Copenhagen 1925), pp. 165–80), see *BRL*, cols. 522 ff. and *IDB* s.v. City, vol. I, pp. 634 and 636. The custom of holding courts before the gate was taken over by the Israelites from the Canaanites. In the Ras Shamra texts there occurs a scene where Dan'el takes his place before the gate and gives justice to the widows and fatherless (19 (I D) I, 19 ff.; 17 (II D) V, 4 ff.).

honestly in a court case. If v. 7 is directed against the judges, v. 10 is also, so that it is a complaint against the judges that in their verdicts they ignore the clear evidence of the innocence of the poor. If it is directed against the rich, which remains the most probable view, the verse describes their indignation against those who support the just cause of the poor.

V. 11 introduces the punishment with לָכֵן (3.11), but before the content of the punishment is mentioned attention is drawn again to an injustice against the poor. בּוֹשַׁסְכֶם is according to its vocalization a poel infinitive with suffix from בשס. This verb is unknown, but the form is obviously connected with the verb בוס (or בסס) 'trample on' (עַל). Most commentators assume that the form was originally written with שׂ, which was then corrected to ס, and that the שׂ was still kept in the text out of respect for the original spelling (cf. Neh. 11.13). But it is not impossible that בשס has arisen by dissimilation from בסס (=בוס), so that the form really is a poel. The allusion, as the following expression shows, is to the harsh exploitation by the rich of their tenants, not to corruption in the law-court. מַשְׂאַת (construct מַשְׂאַת) is the dues which the impoverished small farmers must pay in corn (בַּר is the threshed corn, Gen. 41.35). The punishment consists in the fact that the rich will not enjoy their palaces and vineyards, because, it is implied, the owners will be driven into exile or killed. Houses of hewn stone (גָּזִית 'hewing'; אַבְנֵי גָזִית or simply גָזִית 'ashlar') were more solid and more beautiful than houses of rough stone lumps, not to speak of the huts of sun-dried brick that the poor lived in. Apart from the king the rich also were able to live in houses of hewn stone (Isa. 9.9).[1] Threats of a similar nature to these are found in Deut. 28.30; Mic. 6.15; Zeph. 1.13. Exod. 20.25 forbids the use of hewn stone for an altar. According to 1 Kgs. 5.29–32 and 6.7 Solomon used hewn stone for the foundations of the temple.

V. 12. The punishment is well-founded, because, contrary to what they believe, Yahweh knows fully of their sins. Translate 'I know that your transgressions are many . . .'. עָצוּם 'strong' is also used of numbers, 'numerous'. צרר 'control', 'oppress'. For the thought cf. 2.6; 3.9 f. and 4.1. כֹּפֶר can mean the expiation which a man under certain mitigating circumstances pays in place

---

[1] See further *BRL*, cols. 371 ff., *IDB* s.v. house, vol. 2, p. 657.

of forfeiting his life (e.g. when his ox had gored another, Exod. 21.30), but in a case of manslaughter it was forbidden to let the guilty escape with an expiation (Num. 35.31). Some commentators understand this passage as meaning that the judges have offended against this provision by accepting expiation from the rich, by means naturally of an extra payment to themselves, while the poor have not the means to persuade the judges to let the law remain dormant. It is, however, just as simple to take כֹּפֶר in the sense of 'bribery' (cf. 1 Sam. 12.3), so that it is the corruptness of the judges in general that is spoken of. הִטּוּ 'turn aside', with מִדִּין 'from justice' understood (see Isa. 10.2). They prevent the poor from getting the justice that they are entitled to.

V. 13 is understood by many commentators as an aside, which advises the prudent to be silent in an evil time like this, because one cannot know what risks there are in protesting against the injustices that one sees and hears. Understood in this way the sentence shows an obvious discrepancy with Amos' own mind. The verse does not, however, have to be a piece of advice. It may express the empirical truth that the worldly wise will know how to protect his skin and will not take up the cause of the oppressed (cf. v. 10) in evil times of the sort that are described in the preceding verses. If so, it is not the case that Amos approves of such silence, but quite the contrary.[1]

Vv. 14-15: A renewed demand to seek Yahweh, with hope held out for a part of the people

The summons is so reminiscent of vv. 4-6 as to provide grounds for the conjecture that vv. 14-15 stood originally after vv. 4-6, and that for one reason or another there has been a dislocation of the original order of the verses (cf. on v. 7). In their present place vv. 14-15 break the natural connection between vv. 10-13 and vv. 16 f.

V. 14. 'Seek the good' corresponds in content to the 'seek Yahweh' of vv. 4 and 6. By this Amos thinks first and foremost of the performance of duties to the oppressed and wronged, and aid

---

[1] Sellin (*Das Zwölfprophetenbuch*, pp. 239 f.) translates: 'therefore hymns are silent in this time; for it is a time of disaster'. This understanding of the passage is mentioned with approval by I. Engnell, 'The 'Ebed Yahweh Songs and the Suffering Messiah in "Deutero-Isaiah"', *Bulletin of the John Rylands Library*, 31 (1948), p. 76, n. 2.

to the needy (cf. Isa. 1.17). In the negative form וְאַל־רָע is understood the jussive form of דרש, not the preceding imperative, because this cannot be used with a negative (Gr. § 110a). If the
people fulfil these obligations, they will also obtain Yahweh's
presence with them. Amos takes the opportunity of dissociating
himself from a catch-phrase, which must have run: 'Yahweh is
with us!' It arose from the people's conviction of the unfailing
good fortune which they thought they had evidence of in the
external success of Jeroboam II. For Amos this was only a delu-
sion, and a short respite, before Yahweh would punish them more
seriously than ever before, if they did not repent in time and live
according to his demands. In that case they would be able to
experience that Yahweh was with them, but not otherwise. For
כֵּן with a following כַּאֲשֶׁר cf. Gen. 18.5.

V. 15. The first half-verse rings the changes on the thought in
v. 14a. 'Put justice on its feet' is the opposite of 'cast righteousness to the ground', v. 7. In the second half-verse Amos puts
forward the possibility that Yahweh may have mercy on the
remnant of the people. The uncertainty does not lie in whether
Yahweh will have mercy on them if they repent; the prophet
regards it as dubious whether they really will repent. 'The remnant of Joseph' does not involve the idea that the people (i.e. the
Northern Kingdom) at the time were only an insignificant part of
what they originally had been, but should be understood as
meaning that the prophet expects that at most a fragment of the
people will repent and therefore escape destruction. In relation to
the passages where the complete extermination of the people is
spoken of, it does represent a hope, but one which is heavily
qualified. The concept of a remnant which is preserved takes a
much more prominent place in the preaching of Isaiah than in that
of Amos. It is not impossible that Isaiah took over the idea from
Amos and developed it into a key idea. The imperfect יֶחֱנַן is
formed like a regular pē-guttural verb, instead of יָחֹן (Gr. § 67cc).

Vv. 16–17: A warning of mourning in all the land when Yahweh comes to punish

V. 16. With the introductory לָכֵן a conclusion is not drawn
from what is said in vv. 14–15, but from the warning of punishment in vv. 10 ff. On the original order of the verses see on v. 14.

Yahweh proclaims that lamentation will be heard in all open places and in all streets (cf. Isa. 15.3). הוֹ־הוֹ is an imitation of the cry of the mourners. The most frequent form of the cry of lament is הוֹי (see Jer. 22.18). The last line of v. 16 has given trouble to commentators because of its peculiar grammatical construction. The subject of קְרָאוּ can be אִכָּר 'farmer', if this is taken collectively, but there is also the possibility of taking the word as an object, and making the subject of קְרָאוּ impersonal: 'they call the farmers to mourning'. Which of the two possibilities is chosen depends on the understanding of the parallel expression. In it קְרָאוּ must be understood before מִסְפֵּד, and the verb taken in the sense of 'cry' or 'proclaim': 'and they proclaim mourning to those who are skilled in lamentation'. Most commentators find the construction far-fetched, and correct the text to וְאֶל־מִסְפֵּד. But the MT should not be rejected. The thought is that the deaths are announced to the men and women who by profession are summoned to the mourning. In general these were women (see on 5.1). If one takes the word 'farmer' as object, parallel to 'those that are skilled in lamentation', one is compelled almost inevitably to conclude that the poor farmers used to hire themselves out to mourn the dead. Of this we have no other knowledge. This difficulty is avoided by taking אִכָּר as the subject of the sentence. The verse then declares that mourning will come upon the population of the countryside, as the preceding line described the mourning in the cities, and that the professional mourners are summoned there to take care of the mourning. A great feast of mourning lasted seven days (Gen. 50.10; 1 Sam. 31.13). נְהִי, pausal form נֶהִי 'lament', no doubt the same as the קִינָה of v. 1.

V. 17. In the vineyards, which are traditionally the place for merriment and festivity when the vines are harvested (Judg. 9.27), mourning will now prevail (cf. Isa. 16.10). Yahweh will go through (עבר with בְּ) the people, as he once went through Egypt (Exod. 12.12), and spread mourning around himself.

Vv. 18–27: The day of Yahweh is a day of darkness, because the people lay stress on sacrifices instead of righteousness

V. 18. This section is introduced by a threat against those 'who desire the day of Yahweh'. הוֹי is an interjection which has the nature of a threat (cf. 6.1; Isa. 1.4; 5.8; but not in 1 Kgs. 13.30 and Jer. 22.18, where it is a cry of lamentation, like הוֹי in v. 16).[1] From Amos' rejection of the people's desire for the day of Yahweh we can in the first place conclude that this idea had a central place in the religious expectation of the people, and secondly that this day would according to the current view bring Israel good fortune and victory. The familiarity of the listeners with the idea means, however, that Amos only needs to allude to it, and we are forced to draw our conclusions from elsewhere if we want to look for the origin of this idea. For Gressmann (*Der Messias*, FRLANT N.F. 26, Göttingen 1929, pp. 74 f. and *Der Ursprung der israelitisch-jüdischen Eschatologie*, FRLANT 6, Göttingen 1905, pp. 142 f.) this passage was evidence that already in the time of Amos there existed under the influence of the religions of the surrounding peoples a popular eschatology, which included the expectation of a special day in the future, when Yahweh would reveal himself in all his might and win a decisive victory over all Israel's foes. This understanding of the Old Testament eschatology has been strongly contested by others (among them Mowinckel, see *Psalmenstudien II*, Kristiania 1922), [2] who understand the eschatology as a projection into the future of what was experienced in the cult at the annual New Year Feast, where the Enthronement of Yahweh was celebrated, and his great wonders of the past remembered: the creation together with the defeat of the chaos monster, the election of Israel, the liberation from Egypt, the making of the covenant at Sinai and so on. In the cult these great wonders were experienced again, and the participants joined in ensuring blessing and good fortune for the coming year. When the people were in distress, they put their faith in the coming day of Yahweh, and expected that he would reveal his might as in the past, and save them from their distress. Later the idea of the day of Yahweh, or 'the day', was separated from the cult, and became simply a particular day in the future which was the centre of Israel's eschatological ideas. But Mowinckel thinks that at the time of Amos it was still connected with the cultic feast. Even if Mowinckel were right in his understanding of the relationship

---

[1] Related to the particle הוֹי is אוֹי, which is frequently followed by the preposition לְ: 'woe to' (e.g. Isa. 3.9; 6.5).

[2] For Mowinckel's views on "the day of Yahweh" see also his *He That Cometh*, Oxford 1956, p. 132, and 'Jahves dag', *NTT* 59 (1958), pp. 1–56, 209–29.

between cult and eschatology, and in his conjecture of a special feast of the enthronement of Yahweh, it is open to question whether 'the day of Yahweh' was not already separated from the ancient enthronement feast of Yahweh at the time of Amos, and placed indefinitely in the future. The people perhaps longed for this day of fortune in the future, even when the external circumstances of the people appeared bright as in the time of Amos, after the victories of Jeroboam II.[1] Others would deny completely that there is any connection between 'the day of Yahweh' and this feast, and understand the expression in the light of Arabic usage, where 'day' is often used for 'day of battle' (cf. 'the day of Midian', Isa. 9.3, i.e. the day on which Midian was conquered). But one cannot avoid attempting an explanation of how the idea could have arisen in Israel that Yahweh would one day conquer all his enemies. Through the excavations at Ras Shamra we have found evidence that not only the Babylonians and the Egyptians, but also the Canaanites, who were the teachers of the Israelites in many areas, had a feast with a developed ritual, in which the god's (in the case of the Canaanites Baal's) renewed assumption of royal might was celebrated.[2] The idea of the day of Yahweh occurs very frequently in the prophets (cf. Isa. 2.12 ff.; 13.6 ff.; Joel 2.1 ff.; 4.14 ff.; Zeph. 1.7, 14 ff.).

Whatever the answer to this problem is, it is certain that the people lived under the firm conviction that there was reason to expect every possible good from the future, because they thought that they had fulfilled all that Yahweh demanded, primarily in the feasts and in the sacrifices connected with these. Yahweh could therefore never break his covenant with his people. But Amos goes right against the ideas of the people, and declares that it will be a day of disaster ('it will be darkness and not light'). For the phrase "לָמָּה־זֶּה לָכֶם" cf. לָמָּה לִי חַיִּים Gen. 27.46. זֶה reinforces לָמָּה (Gr. § 136c). Isa. 9.1 uses the words light and darkness in the same metaphorical significance as here of good fortune and disaster. לֹא־אוֹר 'not-light' (Gr. § 152a note 1).

---

[1] The objection can be made to Mowinckel's views that a special feast of the enthronement of Yahweh is not attested anywhere in the Old Testament. On the other hand Mowinckel is right in maintaining that Yahweh's assumption of royal might entered the cult of the Old Testament at the earliest times, cf. the expression יהוה מלך in many psalms.

[2] See on this F. F. Hvidberg, *Graad og Latter i det Gamle Testamente*, Copenhagen 1938, ET *Weeping and Laughter in the Old Testament*, Copenhagen and Leiden 1962.

V. 19 shows by means of images how it will be for the people on that day. To make clear the comparison made by כַּאֲשֶׁר one could insert 'it will be for you as when a man (אִישׁ). . . .' The images employed are used to show that even if a man were lucky enough to escape the danger on the first occasion, fate would nevertheless catch up with him later. Bears can attack both animals and men (1 Sam. 17.34 f.; 2 Kgs. 2.24, cf. Lam. 3.10). The article is used generically before אֲרִי, דֹּב and נָחָשׁ (Gr. § 126m). Inside the houses the light was often very bad, so that a snake hidden inside could easily be overlooked by someone coming in from outside. There are several species of poisonous snakes in Palestine.

V. 20 repeats the conclusion of v. 18, but adds two other words for light and darkness. אָפֵל 'darkness' (only here), נֹגַהּ 'brightness'. The word belongs especially to descriptions of appearances of Yahweh, e.g. Ps. 18.13; Isa. 4.5; Ezek. 1, 10.4; Hab. 3.4, 11; 2 Sam. 23.4.

V. 21. The cause of the catastrophe which threatened the people was to be found in its attachment to a worthless cult instead of an ethical way of life. Yahweh was so far from taking delight in the feasts with all that belonged to them, that on the contrary he hated and indeed detested them (a climax). חַג is the term for the three great pilgrimage feasts: the Feast of Unleavened Bread, the Feast of Weeks and the Feast of Tabernacles, which according to the oldest law should be celebrated at the sanctuary (Ex. 23.14 ff.; Lev. 23.4 ff.; Deut. 16.16).[1] לֹא אָרִיחַ בְּ 'I will not smell at', i.e. take pleasure in (cf. Gen. 8.21). עֲצָרָה or עֲצֶרֶת (plural with suffix עַצְּרֹתֵיכֶם) 'festal assembly'. The word is used especially of the festal assembly on the seventh day of the Feast of Unleavened Bread (Deut. 16.8) and the eighth day of the Feast of Tabernacles (Lev. 23.36); here it is used in a general sense.

V. 22. The MT must be translated: 'For when you bring your burnt offerings and your cereal offerings, I have no pleasure in them.' Some commentators wish to delete the words כִּי אִם תַּעֲלוּ לִי עֹלוֹת, but without good reasons; it is better to assume that something has fallen out in the line (cf. *BH*); in that case מִנְחֹתֵיכֶם may be the object of אֶרְצֶה. עֹלָה is a burnt offering in which the whole

---

[1] The basic meaning of חַג is probably the cultic dance at the festivals, but this meaning is completely lost in Hebrew. The case is somewhat similar in Arabic, where the word is used of the pilgrimage to Mecca.

animal is offered on the altar, and is burnt up completely. It is
also called a כָּלִיל 'whole offering'. In a שֶׁלֶם 'peace offering' only
a part of the animal, usually the fat parts, was put on the altar
(1 Sam. 2.15), while the rest was consumed by the man or men
who offered it in a sacrificial feast; the same was the case with the
זֶבַח 'sacrifice', i.e. a slain offering (v. 25 and 4.4) whereas מִנְחָה is
the bloodless sacrifice (RSV cereal offering). The word was
originally a description for an offering in general (Gen. 4.4), but
was used later especially of the vegetable offerings; so also here.
מְרִיא 'fatstock', here in the plural, as in Isa. 1.11.

V. 23. At the feasts song and music were heard, but Yahweh
did not take any pleasure in these either. מֵעָלַי implies that they
are to be removed so that they do not weigh upon him like a
burden (cf. Isa. 1.14). The command הָסֵר is directed to the people
(notice the singular suffix in the following words). The songs are
to Yahweh only noise and din (הָמוֹן). The songs were accompanied by harp music. נֵבֶל or גֶבֶל 'a harp'. זִמְרָה 'the sound of the
music of strings'. It is difficult to say more precisely how far these
songs were similar to the psalms that are preserved to us in the
Old Testament from the cult of the pre-exilic temple. Perhaps
they were songs and music which had become degenerate under
the influence of the cult of Baal (cf. Exod. 32.17–19). But even if
the songs which Amos attacked were in content different from the
psalms in the Psalter, v. 23 is indirectly evidence that the psalms
belonged to the cult. For Yahweh's rejection of the prayers of
Israel cf. Isa. 1.15.

V. 24 stresses Yahweh's demand for righteousness as that
which he values rather than the cultic feasts of the people. We
can show the contrast with the preceding verse by translating ׳ by
'but'. That we have here a demand from Yahweh can be seen
from the jussive form יִגַּל (from גלל, niphal 'roll down', intransitive). What is implied in the images used depends on our understanding of כְּנַחַל אֵיתָן, since the meaning of the adjective is disputed. Some translate it by 'permanent', 'lasting'. The image
would then mean that the righteousness of the people, in contrast
to the streams which only flow in the rainy season (cf. Jer. 15.18
אַכְזָב 'a stream which fails'), will flow for ever. Others, however,
keep the meaning 'strong' for אֵיתָן, as expressing the strength and
irresistibility which their righteous dealings will always have. In
support of this translation of אֵיתָן reference can be made to the

Hebrew of Sirach 40.13, where the same expression is found. In either case מִשְׁפָּט and צְדָקָה are the justice and righteousness which the people are to practise, not Yahweh's punishing righteousness, as some have suggested with reference to the meaning of מִשְׁפָּט in Isa. 5.16 and the image in Isa. 10.22 ('destruction is decreed, overflowing with righteousness'). The first sense of 'justice' and 'righteousness' fits much better here. The passage has a parallel in Isa. 1.16 f., where the prophet after a powerful utterance against the sacrifices of the people ends by demanding that they should cease from evil, and instead care for what is right.

V. 25. For the correct understanding of this and the following two verses, which are among the most difficult in the whole book, it is important to realize that the emphasis rests on the words זְבָחִים and מִנְחָה, which are placed at the beginning of the sentence, and not on לִי (me, Yahweh), as if he were contrasted with other gods. We can further establish immediately that the question in the verse is meant to be answered in the negative (on הַ see Gr. § 150d). If the prophet's listeners had to concede that Israel did not offer Yahweh sacrifices in the forty years of the wandering in the wilderness, which could be regarded as a time when the people were under the full care of Yahweh (see 2.9 ff.), they would be able to realize that sacrifices had no influence on Yahweh's good will towards the people, and therefore were not a necessary part of the people's worship of him.

The presupposition of Amos' question to his listeners must be that he regarded it as a fact that the people did not sacrifice during the wilderness period. If his listeners had not agreed with him, or had there existed a tradition to the opposite effect, Amos would have run the risk of being contradicted, and thereby have weakened his argument. But does Amos mean that Moses did not promulgate laws about the cult at all? This is maintained by many commentators, who quote as a parallel to this passage Jer. 7.22, which runs: 'in the day I brought your fathers out of Egypt, I did not speak to them or command them concerning burnt offerings and sacrifices. But this command I gave them, "Obey my voice, and I will be your God, and you shall be my people; and walk in all the way that I command you, that it may be well with you."' Even if no more can be concluded from Jeremiah's language than that God had not *demanded* sacrifice (but not that the people did not offer it), the passage is in conflict with the Pentateuch, particularly the so-called priestly laws which attribute to Moses all the rules about the cult, and assert that the sacrificial system began with Aaron's first sacrifice (Lev. 9). If Amos means to say the same about the Mosaic period, it follows that the Pentateuch cannot have been recognized as canonical at this time. Other commentators, however, think that Amos does not refer at all to the question of whether Yahweh prescribed cultic laws to the people through Moses, but simply fastens on the fact that during the wilderness period the people *could* not offer sacrifice, and uses this as evidence that sacrifices are useless, because everyone knew that the wilderness period was in fact a time of God's favour. This interpretation does not therefore exclude the idea that Moses gave the cultic laws, but these could not come into force until after the entry into Canaan. Historically the situation is that all Semitic peoples offered sacrifice. Israel therefore probably also employed sacrifices before the wilderness period, but during this period must have restricted its sacrifices very considerably because of circumstances. Wilderness nomads could not take cattle with them, and only small numbers of sheep and goats, and could not in any case have allowed themselves to sacrifice in the quantities which the laws of the Pentateuch prescribe. After the entry into Canaan the Israelites offered all the sacrifices which went with the seasons of the year, and imitated the cultus of the Canaanites. The unfortunate consequences of this were a thorn in the flesh to the prophets, so that it is understandable that in their polemic against the cult they refer to the wilderness period as an ideal time.

V. 26. In this verse the difficulties begin with the first word וּנְשָׂאתֶם, which allows of several interpretations: (1) The verb is taken as future, parallel with וְהִגְלֵיתִי in v. 27: 'so you shall carry ...'; (2) The verb is taken as introducing a conditional clause, which is continued by והגליתי in v. 27: 'if you carry ..., I will take you ...'; (3) ונשאתם is taken as past, but as a contrast with and answer to v. 25: 'No! But you have carried ...'; (4) The verb is taken as parallel to הגשתם in v. 25, so that the whole verse is a question, which like v. 25 presupposes a negative answer. Irrespective of which possibility is chosen, the Massoretic vocalization of סִכּוּת and of כִּיּוּן must be regarded as misleading. סִכּוּת should not be taken as meaning 'hut' or 'tent' (LXX and the other translations seem to have read it as סֻכַּת), so that the

thought is of a holy tent for the deity ('the king'). The vocalization is adapted from the word שִׁקּוּץ 'abomination', a generally
used contemptuous designation of foreign idols (e.g. 2 Kgs.
23.13; Deut. 29.16).[1] Originally it certainly read Sakkut, which
is an alternative name of the Assyrian and Babylonian god Ninib
(Saturn). Similarly כִּיּוּן is not a common noun meaning 'foot-
stool' or 'statue' (cf. the root כּוּן), but has been given the vowels
of שִׁקּוּץ and is in reality a proper noun Kaiwan or Kewan, which
also corresponds to the planet Saturn (cf. the LXX: 'Ραιφαν,
resulting from a miswriting of Καιφαν).[2] The two names Sakkut
and Kaiwan occur together along with the names of other stars
in an Assyrian text (see H. Zimmern, Beiträge zur Kenntnis der
babylonischen Religion, Leipzig 1901, p. 10).

    Grammatically there is no problem in taking וּנְשָׂאתֶם of the
future (interpretation 1), for וְהִגְלֵיתִי must of course be understood
as future. But the transition from v. 25 to v. 26 is very abrupt, and
less easily intelligible to the listeners or readers than in v. 27,
where we must in any case suppose a sharp change; but in this
case the sense is more easily grasped, because the verb וְהִגְלֵיתִי itself points immediately in the direction of a threat.[3] On the other
hand it is more of a problem that on this interpretation we must
take נָשָׂא in the sense of 'carry away' (in captivity), i.e. the Israelites must experience the humiliation of themselves carrying away
their images to deliver them to the victors in their home country.
The general custom seems to have been that the victors carried
away the images of gods with them as trophies (Hos. 10.5; Isa.
46.2; Jer. 48.7; 49.3). Both this and several of the other interpretations given presuppose the presence of the Assyrian astral cult
in the time of Amos, but this is scarcely a serious objection, for it
is certainly impossible to claim that the Assyrian astral cult first
gained admittance with the people of foreign origin who settled
in the Northern Kingdom after the deportation in 722 (2 Kgs.
17.24–34, cf. 21.3 ff.). The second interpretation suffers from the
fault that the threat of deportation was only based on a hypo-
thetical worship of false gods. The words צַלְמֵיכֶם, מַלְכְּכֶם and

---

[1] An analogy to such an alteration is found in the form עַשְׁתֹּרֶת, in which the name of
the goddess Astarte has been given the vowels from בֹּשֶׁת 'shame'.

[2] In Acts 7.43 the name is corrupted further to 'Ρέμφαν or 'Ρόμφαν or yet further
forms (see Nestle).

[3] In Hos. 8.14 and 10.14 too a consecutive perfect introduces the penalty, but not after
a question as here.

אֱלֹהֵיכֶם, which some would without justification delete, show that the apostasy had already happened. According to the third interpretation, which requires וּנְשָׂא to mean 'carry in procession', Amos reproves the people for their Assyrian astral cult right back in the wilderness period. How far Amos may have counted on the possibility of Assyrian influence so early it is perhaps not very useful to discuss, but the accusation itself in any case does not fit Amos' view of the wilderness period as a time of grace (2.9 f.). The fourth interpretation also takes וּנְשָׂא in the sense of 'carry in procession', and makes the passage refer to the Assyrian astral cult at the time of Amos. He points out to the Israelites that this was unknown at the time of the wilderness period, when they also did not offer all the sacrifices that they now do, and threatens them therefore with deportation. It is perhaps surprising that Amos speaks of this foreign cult so briefly, but it is understandable in view of the brevity of the book in general. The plural צַלְמֵיכֶם 'your images' seems strange in apposition to the preceding word כִּיּוּן; the singular would undeniably be easier. It is difficult to make it refer to both the preceding words. Some commentators less convincingly understand the word as the Aramaean god Ṣalm, known from the Tema inscriptions (see *NSI*, pp. 195 f., *KAI*, Nos. 228–9), who is supposed again to be Saturn. 'The star of your god' can only be understood as referring to some kind of image of the god. The translation 'your star-god' is not grammatically defensible.

V. 27. Deportation beyond Damascus could only mean that the Assyrians would carry away the population of the Northern Kingdom. There is no other power that could wish to deport them in this direction. מֵהָלְאָה לְ literally 'belonging to (מִן) that which is beyond in respect to' = 'beyond'. Acts 7.43 thought of the captivity in Babylon and therefore altered 'Damascus' to 'Babylon' without noticing that 'beyond' then becomes meaningless.

Because of the difficulties which are connected with the understanding of vv. 26 f., it cannot be decided with certainty what the sin of the people is. Probably it is their degenerate cult and lack of ethical living. This gives no final answer to the disputed problem whether the prophets have rejected the cultus completely, or only so far as the people valued it as a means of changing Yahweh's mind in spite of their inadequate fulfilment of the law's ethical demands. The question can perhaps never be finally answered, because the threats against the cult are shaped by polemic, and precisely for that reason may sound more absolute than is really intended. If we only considered the way they are phrased in Amos and looked at the passages out of context, we would find it difficult to deny that he was a convinced opponent of all cult; but the problem occurs again in several others of the earlier prophets, where attacks against the worship of the people are just as sharp (Isa. 1.10–17; Hos. 6.6; Mic. 6.6–8, cf. also Jer. 6.19 f.; 7.1–15, 21–23), and yet features are found in these prophets which show that it is impossible to say that they have rejected every form of cult. Isaiah for example is called as a prophet in the sanctuary and purified by a cultic act, before he can begin his activity as a prophet (Isa. 6). It is therefore hard to suppose that he was an absolute opponent of every form of cult. He probably regarded sacrifices as a natural expression of the people's worship of Yahweh, but denied that they have an expiatory or mitigatory influence on him. Something similar may have been the case with the other prophets, so that the passages of polemic against sacrifice are directed against the faulty evaluation of sacrifices in relation to the central thought of the covenant with Yahweh, which can be expressed in his demand for righteousness and integrity.[1]

CHAPTER SIX

Vv. 1–7: A declaration of punishment against the heedless who live in luxury and revelry

The construction of the passage is similar to that of 5.18–27. It begins with a cry of woe (הוֹי) and concludes with a declaration of deportation. Corresponding to the mention of the day of Yahweh in 5.18 and 20, which the people expected would be light, it is said here in v. 3 that they thrust the day of misfortune from themselves.

V. 1. According to the MT the cry of woe is for those who are

---

[1] See further on this question the standard works on the religion of the Old Testament, and W. O. E. Oesterley, *Sacrifices in Ancient Israel*, London 1937, especially pp. 191 ff., and H. Ringgren, *Sacrifice in the Bible*, London 1962.

carefree in Zion and those who are secure upon the mountain of
Samaria. Although the parallelism could not be better, many
commentators object to the text, because they doubt the genuineness of the mention of Zion. They point out that Amos' preaching is not elsewhere directed to Judah, and further assert that the
following description only applies to a single city (see v. 8), and
this must, as the expression 'the ruin of Joseph' in v. 6 shows, be
Samaria. Some propose therefore to alter צִיוֹן to עִיר 'the city',
others to delete completely השאנים בציון as a later addition. We
should nevertheless keep the MT, which must be understood as
showing the threat worked out with poetic parallelism against the
two capital cities. Amos knows that in both cities there is a way
of life which awakens Yahweh's wrath; nevertheless in what follows, where he goes into details, he keeps to Samaria, which was
after all the capital of the kingdom where he was to prophesy.
השאנים and הבטחים are not said of those who really have reason to
feel themselves secure and safe, but of those who live heedlessly
in a wanton and disgraceful manner (cf. Isa. 32.9).[1] On Zion see
1.2, and on the mountain of Samaria 4.1. נְקֻבֵי רֵאשִׁית must mean
'the most prominent men from the best of peoples'. נקב literally
'pierce', so 'mark' (by piercing), i.e. 'make recognizable'. The
passive participle can therefore be used of those who are marked
out or stressed in relation to the great undistinguished multitude,
i.e. of the prominent men (cf. Arabic *nakīb* 'leader', 'prince').
רֵאשִׁית is used here of the first and best part (cf. of Amalek Num.
24.20). The whole expression refers to how they understood
themselves, but has of course an ironic sound on the lips of Amos.
The conclusion of the verse is a relative clause: 'and to whom the
house of Israel come'. To make sense of this we must supply 'to
honour them', or perhaps rather: 'so that they shall deal with
their lawsuits' (cf. Exod. 18.16; 2 Sam. 15.4). It is of course a
difficulty that something so important should be understood, but
it is preferable to *BH*'s suggestion וְכֵאלֹהִים הֵם לְבֵית יְ 'and they
are like gods to the house of Israel'. The reference would in that
case be to the divine position of the king in ancient Israel (Ps.
45.7). 'The house of Israel' is perhaps used of the whole people,
not just of the Northern Kingdom.

---

[1] This understanding is to be preferred to the translation 'those who are proud over
Zion', so that the reference is to a north Israelite victory over Judah, perhaps the occasion
of 2 Kgs. 14.8 ff. (as is argued by A. Weiser, *Die Prophetie des Amos*, p. 230).

V. 2 alludes to three cities and some events in their history
which were well known to the listeners. For us there are diffi-
culties in establishing to what the references allude. כַּלְנֵה is the
same as the כַּלְנוֹ of Isa. 10.9. The city probably lay a little north of
Aleppo. It is not therefore the same as the Babylonian Calneh of
Gen. 10.10, but is probably the city that is called by the Assyrians
Kullani or Gullani. It was conquered by Tiglath Pileser in 738
(*ANET*, p. 282).

Hamath (now called Ḥama) also lies in northern Syria, by the
river Orontes, a couple of hundred kilometres north of Damascus.
The district ruled by the city extended a good distance to the
south (according to 2 Kgs. 23.33 and 25.21 Riblah belonged to
'the land of Hamath'). From the time of David a king of Hamath
is known called Toʻi, who brought to David gifts of tribute
(2 Sam. 8.9 f.). Some commentators think, however, that Hamath
in this passage is not the city on the Orontes, but Ḥamat-Ṣoba
(cf. 2 Chron. 8.3 f.), which is assumed to have been situated south
of Damascus. In distinction from Ḥamat-Ṣoba the city on the
Orontes is called 'Hamath the great' as here (on the omission of
the article with the adjective see Gr. § 126y). In the Assyrian
sources it is reported that Shalmaneser III conducted a campaign
against Syria in the years 854, 849 and 846 B.C. and fought with
different kings, among them Irḥulini of Hamath, whom the
Assyrian king claims to have beaten thoroughly (*AOT*, pp. 340–3,
ANET, pp. 278 f.). The effect of the victory was, however, only
brief. It appears from hieroglyphic Hittite inscriptions from
Hamath that Irḥulini kept the throne and was later succeeded by
his son.[1] At the beginning of the eighth century an Aramaean
called Zakir seized power in the city, but apart from this we know
nothing of this period except what the so-called Zakir inscription
recounts (see *AOT*, pp. 443 f., *ANET*, pp. 501 f.). The next we
hear of the history of Hamath is from the Assyrian annals, which
report that Tiglath-Pileser III in 738 incorporated nineteen of the
provinces of Hamath into the Assyrian kingdom (*AOT*, p. 346,
ANET, p. 282). However, Hamath was not wholly brought to
its knees, for in 720 Sargon slew Yaubidi (or Ilubidi) king of
Hamath, and had him flayed as a punishment, because he had been
the instigator of a revolt against Assyria, into which several

---

[1] See B. Hrozny, *Les Inscriptions hittites hiéroglyphiques*, II, Prague 1934, pp. 297 ff.

7—B.A.

Syrian cities were drawn. The population of Hamath was incorporated into the Assyrian army or deported, some to Samaria
(2 Kgs. 17.24–30; 18.33 f. and 19.12 f.); in return 6,300 Assyrians
settled in Hamath (*AOT*, pp. 348–50, *ANET*, pp. 284 f.). In the
Greek period the city was named ᾽Επιφάνεια.[1]

The Philistine city Gath was the only one of the five great
Philistine cities which was not mentioned in 1.6–8. According to
1. Sam. 17.4 the city was the home town of Goliath (cf. 2 Sam.
21.19 f.). For a time David sought refuge in it with king Achish
(1 Sam. 21.10 ff.; 27.11). Later David made use of men of Gath in
his bodyguard (2 Sam. 15.18). The city was probably incorporated into the kingdom of Judah towards the end of the reign of
Solomon; it was in any case regarded as belonging to this kingdom when Hazael the Aramaean king besieged and captured the
city c. 815 B.C., and then threatened to march against Jerusalem
(2 Kgs. 12.18 f.). On this occasion Gath returned to Philistine
control. According to 2 Chron. 26.6 Uzziah made an attempt to
reconquer it, and pulled down the city walls of both Gath and
Ashdod. Both cities were also besieged and conquered by Sargon
in 711 (*AOT*, pp. 350 f., *ANET*, p. 286). From this time on Gath
plays no further part in history. The city was probably identical
with Tell eṣ-ṣāfi (on the history of the city and theories of its
location see further *BRL* s.v. Gath, cols. 170 ff. and *IDB* s.v.
Gath, vol. 2, pp. 355 f.).

Commentators are not agreed on why these cities are quoted as
examples for the listeners. Some say that they are produced as
examples of good fortune and prosperity, and that the Israelites
are intended to realize that they themselves are specially favoured
by Yahweh, because these mighty and prosperous cities are no
better off, and their territory no greater, than that of the Israelites (הממלכות האלה are in that case the kingdoms of Israel and
Judah). The harsh punishment to which the Israelites are sentenced is due to their privileged position (cf. for the thought
2.9–16 and 3.2). Others argue that the context is evidence that
these cities are quoted as places that once were grand and power-

---

[1] In the years 1931–8, excavations were undertaken in Hamath by a Danish team led by
Harald Ingholt under the aegis of the Carlsberg Foundation. See Ingholt's reports,
Rapport préliminaire sur la première campagne des fouilles de Hama, dansk Videnskabernes
Selskabs archæologisk-kunsthistorisk Meddelelser I, 3, Copenhagen 1934, and *Rapport
préliminaire sur sept campagnes de fouilles à Hama en Syrie, 1932–1938*, ibid., 3 i, 1940.

ful, but have now perished. When the Israelites realize that their
own country cannot be compared with these, they must perceive
what they can expect. The prophet then gives the reason for his
declaration of punishment, pointing out to them their dissolute
way of life (vv. 3–6). This interpretation, however, demands two
textual alterations. After הַטּוֹבִים there should stand אתם 'you', and
at the end of the verse the suffixes must be exchanged, so that the
text runs: 'is your territory greater than their territory?'. The
answer to this must of course be 'no'. Since this text could have
given offence at a later period, it is not inconceivable that the
original text was deliberately altered, and so became meaningless.
This is the interpretation most commentators give to the verse,
but they also assert that it must be secondary, since reference is
made to events after the death of Amos. They think that the conquest of Hamath in 720 and of Gath in 711 are alluded to. But it is
not necessary to think of such late events. The reference could be
to Shalmaneser III's campaign against Hamath in the years 854–
846 (see above); on this occasion Calneh also lay in the battle area
(it was later conquered again in 738, see Isa. 10.9), and the capture of Gath may be Hazael's conquest of the city in 815. There
was still a vivid memory of these events at the time of Amos, so
that he can refer to them to warn Israel what they must expect if
they do not repent in time. The people, however, have put their
trust in the victories of Jeroboam II (v. 13), and thought that
there was peace and no danger.

V. 3 continues the characterization which began after the word
הוֹי in v. 1. הַמְנַדִּים comes from נדה, which is only found here and in
Isa. 66.5. It is related to נדד 'flee'; here it must mean 'remove',
'thrust away', i.e. they feel themselves secure, and push away the
thought of the day of misfortune in the belief that it will never
come. לְ before the object is reminiscent of the construction in
Aramaic (cf. Gr. § 117n). Some want to correct the text, in view
of the reading οἱ εὐχόμενοι in some manuscripts of the LXX
(see *BH*), to מְנַדְּרִים 'who make a vow', i.e. to prevent the day of
misfortune. MT should be preferred. The parallel half-verse 'you
bring near the seat of violence' may mean that in place of making
room for justice they let oppression rule, which will soon call
down a righteous punishment on them. Otherwise one could
understand 'the rule of violence' as the coming of the conquering
king, which they only succeed in bringing nearer, although they

want to push the day of misfortune away from them. *BH*'s alteration of שֶׁבֶת to שְׁנַת ('the year of violence') is no improvement.

V. 4 introduces a description of their feasts with a continuation
in vv. 5 and 6. The feasts which are here described should according to some be understood not as banquets in the houses of the
rich, but as sacrificial feasts in the temples (cf. 2.8); but the mention of beds of ivory is an argument that they are held in private
houses (cf. 'their couches'). In earliest times men sat at table
(Gen. 27.19; Judg. 19.6; 1 Sam. 20.5; 1 Kgs. 13.20); here the
custom of reclining at table is mentioned for the first time. Amos
treats it as a sign of decadence that the rich recline at table at their
feasts. Out in the countryside it had certainly not gained accept-
ance at this time. At the time of the New Testament it had become a general custom, so that no one is offended by it (see Matt.
9.10; 26.7, etc.). 'Beds of ivory' must mean beds with ivory in-
laid in the woodwork (cf. on 3.15).[1] סָרוּחַ is used in Ex. 26.13 of
tent-curtains which hang down; here it must describe how the
rich recline, comfortably relaxed, on their couches during the
feasts. The meat is the tastiest that they can get: choice lamb and
calves from their feeding-stalls (מַרְבֵּק literally the place where they
are tied up (to be fed), cf. Arabic *rabaqa* 'tie up'). It hurts the
feelings of the shepherd of Tekoa that good animals are used for
feasts of this sort.

V. 5. At the feasts singing and music could be heard (cf. Isa.
5.12). The verb פרט only occurs here in the Old Testament. In
several of the related languages it is known in the sense of 'pull
off', and in particular in Arabic in the sense of knocking fruit down
(cf. פֶּרֶט in Lev. 19.10 of the picked or fallen berry); it has been
thought that the verb should mean 'pull into strands'. It is
better, however, to compare the Arabic *fāriṭ* 'improviser', and
so make the meaning 'improvise'. Others again prefer the meaning 'sing' (hymns, etc.), which is known from Samaritan (see the
lexica). עַל־פִּי הַנָּבֶל must mean 'to the sound of the harp', since it
does not make sense to translate 'upon the mouth of the harp'.
V. 5b can only be translated: 'like David they invent instruments'. This seems strange, since there is no reason to stress that
they invent them at the feasts. כְּלִי cannot, however, mean
'melodies', as some have suggested; it would be better to read

---

[1] Beds of ivory are mentioned among Hezekiah's gifts to Sennacherib (*AOT*, p. 354, *ANET*, p. 288).

כָּל־ 'all sorts of' or to conjecture that the word כְּלִי has been added under the influence of 1 Chron. 23.5 and of Neh.12.36, where it is said that David had musical instruments made. David was especially remembered for his talent of composition and for his lyre-playing (cf. 1 Sam. 16.23, and the headings of the psalms). One cannot conclude from this passage that David was supposed to have composed gay secular songs too. The prophet only mocks at their drunken attempts to appear like another David.

V. 6. בְּמִזְרְקֵי יַיִן must be translated 'from winebowls'; it could only be translated 'they drink wine from bowls' if the text were corrected to בְּמִזְרָקִים יַיִן or to בְּמִזְרָק יַיִן. One view is that their offence consists in not being satisfied with drinking wine from goblets in small quantities, but drinking it from the bowl. But the meaning is certainly that they have committed an offence by using sacrificial bowls, which it was not permissible to drink from.[1] The LXX perhaps read יַיִן מְזֻקָּק or מְזֻקַּק יַיִן 'strained wine' (the latter construction would be an example of an adjective in the construct with a noun, Gr. § 128w). In the expression שָׁתָה בְ 'drink of' the בְ is instrumental, cf. Gen. 44.5 (not introducing the content, as in Prov. 9.5). Anointing the skin with oil is a feature of the care of the skin which is only given up for mourning (2 Sam. 14.2). Anointing is therefore a sign of gladness, and is part of the preparations for a festival (Isa. 61.3; Eccles. 9.8; Ps. 23.5; 45.8); but Amos is sarcastic at their expense because they have demanded nothing less than the best oil. The word רֵאשִׁית could, however, also be taken in the meaning 'firstfruits', and their sin would then be that they have anointed themselves with the firstfruits, which were due to Yahweh (Num. 18.12). The verb מָשַׁח 'rub', 'anoint' is here used in a reflexive sense with an object: 'they anoint themselves with'. They have only been concerned with pleasure, and have not worried about (נֶחְלוּ, literally 'be ill about', niphal of חלה) the impending danger which threatened the people. שֵׁבֶר or שֶׁבֶר means literally 'breach' (for example in a wall), so 'devastation', 'ruin' (Isa. 1.28). This latter sense fits very well here. Some commentators, however, take it as referring to the miserable state that the people had gradually fallen into as a result of the moral corruption of the upper classes. Others again think that שֵׁבֶר alludes to the division of the kingdoms. In support

---

[1] On the different types of bowls see *BRL* s.v. Keramik, cols. 314 ff., *IDB* s.v. pottery, vol. 3, pp. 846 ff.

of this view it can be pointed out that Amos regarded this event as a national catastrophe (see on 9.11). The word 'Joseph' shows that this utterance is directed at the Northern Kingdom.

V. 7 contains the punishment. It is said with irony that they are to keep their leading position in the disaster—with the implication that they will walk at the head of those deported. With a wordplay between סָר and סְרוּחִים it is said finally that the mirth of those who lounge about shall cease. מַרְזֵחַ, construct מִרְזַח 'loud cry', sometimes a cry of mourning (Jer. 16.5), sometimes a cry of joy. Here it could reasonably be translated 'clamour'. Koehler's dictionary (KB, p. 566) renders it by 'banquet', 'cult festival', cf. in the LXX θίασος (Jer. 16.5).

Vv. 8–11: Yahweh swears that he will devastate Samaria completely

V. 8. After v. 7 has proclaimed the deportation of the people as a punishment for the degeneracy of the city, Yahweh makes the threat yet more serious by his oath. He swears by himself בְּנַפְשׁוֹ, with a sense similar to בְּקָדְשׁוֹ 4.2. מְתָאֵב should properly mean 'desire', but from the context cannot mean anything other than 'abhor', i.e. מְתָעֵב. It is perhaps a tendentious distortion of a strong expression at which offence was later taken, and which it was desired to mitigate. If it is a mishearing, it must come from a late period, since א and ע were sharply distinguished from one another in pronunciation in the pre-exilic period.[1] גְּאוֹן יַעֲקֹב 'the pride of Jacob' either means his conceited boasting, or the object of his boasting. In fact there is no great difference between the two meanings, since the allusion is to the pride of the people at the external and internal successes of the period of Jeroboam II (cf. v. 13). Some conclude from v. 8b that גָאוֹן refers to the magnificent palaces, but the punishment which is in prospect fits the first interpretation just as well. הִסְגִּיר 'give up' means to give completely into the power of the enemy (cf. 1.6). עִיר must be Samaria, even though the word does not have the article. מְלֹאָהּ 'the fulness of it' means all that is in it.

---

[1] Sellin (*Das Zwölfprophetenbuch*, p. 246) suggests that the copyist had in mind Ps. 47.5, where Yahweh loves (אהב) the pride of Jacob (גאון).

Vv. 9–10 describe a scene in which plague or some other infection further devastates the people, after many have already fallen in battle or been deported (v. 7). V. 9 says that even if there were ten left in a house, they would all die of a pestilence. This implies firstly that there were originally even more in the house, and secondly that it is one of the rich men's palaces spoken of in v. 8, since none of the houses of the poor could have room for so many inhabitants. V. 10 speaks of one single survivor, but the whole picture is in any case very confused, because we cannot decide definitely who is the subject of the different verbs, and to whom the different suffixes refer. The view can be taken that the suffixes in the three words דּוֹדוֹ, נְשָׂאוֹ and מְסָרְפוֹ refer to one of the dead, and that the situation is the following: a relation of one of the dead goes into the house, accompanied by a corpse-burner to carry the body out of the house. Inside the house he discovers that in the innermost part there is still one man left who has escaped death. To the question whether there are more who are alive the survivor answers no. At once the man who has come into the house hastens to tell him to be silent, because he should not say more than this short answer, nor for example begin to lament and upbraid Yahweh because he has slain so many, or perhaps begin to praise Yahweh because he is still alive. The assumption must be that even to mention the name of Yahweh in such a situation can be dangerous, because it will lead Yahweh to notice that someone is still alive, and encourage him to slay this one also. The clause which is introduced by כִּי is to be understood as the prophet's interpretation of the word 'Hush'. It would also be possible that the conversation is held between the relation of the dead man and the corpse-burner, and that it takes place while one of them is inside the house, and the other stands outside and asks whether there are more inside to be carried out. The warning against mentioning the name of Yahweh would in that case be in respect of these two, who until now have escaped, and is of course the commentary of the prophet. דּוֹד 'father's brother, uncle', here perhaps simply 'kinsman'. The thought is no doubt that the sons and brothers, who would be the most appropriate to carry this out, have already died. מְסָרְפוֹ is equivalent to מְשָׂרְפוֹ, literally 'his burner'; some understand it as referring to one who burns fragrant materials in honour of the dead (cf. 2 Chron. 16.14; 21.19; Jer. 34.5). It is more probable to assume that at a time of plague corpses could be burned as an exceptional measure, to limit the danger of infection, or because no burials could take place outside the city by reason of a siege. מסרפו is then 'he who burns him'.[1] On cremation see further on 2.1. עֲצָמִים here 'bones of a dead man'; in this sense it is most often the feminine plural that is used (e.g. Gen. 50.25). *יַרְכָה 'flank', 'side'; the dual means 'inside', 'the innermost place' (in a house or other place, cf. 1 Sam. 24.4 of a cave). אֶפֶס 'cease' = 'no!' הַס an exclamatory particle: 'be silent!' לא with ל and infinitive: 'it does not do to', 'it is not appropriate to'. הִזְכִּיר with בְּ: 'call upon' (cf. Isa. 48.1).

V. 11 refers again like v. 8 to the devastation of the city through the effects of war. כִּי should not be pressed, so that it gives the reason for what precedes. It serves as a transition particle between the two sections. After מִצֻּוֶה there is no object to express who receives the order; this object is the same as the subject of the following verb הִכָּה. V. 14 allows us to conjecture that it is the people of Assyria who are in mind here (for the thought cf. Isa. 10.6). The concise form of the expression is due to the fact that in the Semitic languages one can take together a command and its carrying out. Instead of saying 'he tells him to smite, and he smites', one can say 'he tells him, and he smites'. רְסִיס*, plural רְסִיסִים 'fragments', 'ruins' (hapax legomenon). בְּקִיעַ 'split', 'rift' (only here and Isa. 22.9). The verb הִכָּה takes two objects: he smites the house into ruins. 'The great house' and 'the little house' do not allude to the kingdoms of Israel and Judah (so the Targum), but to the palaces of the rich and the cottages of the poor.

Vv. 12–14: The moral degeneracy and pride of the people will cause Yahweh to punish Israel through a foreign nation

V. 12. The first question is to be answered in the negative, since horses cannot run on rocks.[2] So we expect that the next question too will require an answer in the negative. But the text of MT expects a positive answer, since it is precisely the case that

---

[1] According to a Jewish tradition the word means 'mother's brother'; this is no doubt derived from the parallelism with דּוֹדוֹ. This meaning is supported however, by B. Felsenthal, 'Zur Bibel und Grammatik', in G. A. Kohut, *Semitic Studies in Memory of Alexander Kohut*, Berlin 1897, pp. 133 ff.

[2] It is well-known that at the time of the Settlement the Israelites kept to the hill-country and avoided battles in the lowland, where they were bound to be defeated by the horsedrawn chariots of the Canaanites. These could not operate in the hill country, and for this reason the God of Israel came to be treated as a mountain-god (cf. 1 Kgs. 20.23).

one does plough with oxen. A suitable text is obtained by dividing the consonants בבקרים into two words: בַּבָּקָר יָם, so that the question runs: 'does one plough the sea with oxen?' This reading has the further advantage of avoiding the plural form of בָּקָר, which is a collective word. The mistake in the Massoretic vocalization is understandable, in that originally no division was made between words in a consonantal text. כִּי in the next line is translated 'since'. The two images employed in v. 12a are intended to express how unnaturally the people have reversed the true order of right and wrong. Yahweh demands that righteousness should receive its material reward, while the profligate are punished; but the rich men and the corrupt judges set up a challenge to Yahweh by allowing violence and injustice to flourish at the expense of the community. Yahweh's punishment too will therefore not fail. רֹאשׁ is a poisonous plant, and so comes to mean 'poison'. The etymology of the word is uncertain. For the thought cf. 5.7.

V. 13. The determinate adjective הַשְּׂמֵחִים is in apposition to the subject implied in הֲפַכְתֶּם. The verse contains a sarcastic allusion to the conquests of Jeroboam II in Transjordan, which are narrated in 2 Kgs. 14.25: he restored the territory of Israel from the region near (literally the entrance to) Hamath and down to the Sea of the Arabah (i.e. the Dead Sea). Amos mentions two cities within this territory: Lodebar and Qarnaim.[1] He distorts the name of the first, which is known from 2 Sam. 17.27, where it is written לֹא דְבָר, or 2 Sam. 9.4 f., where it is spelt לוֹ דְבָר (cf. perhaps לִדְבָר in Josh. 13.26). Amos calls it לֹא דָבָר 'not anything', to show how little value he attaches to the conquest. קַרְנַיִם (literally 'the two horns') is known from 1 Macc. 5.43, and is probably the same as Ashteroth Qarnaim in Gen. 14.5. Horns usually symbolize strength; the name here is a sarcastic allusion to the supposed strength of the people.

V. 14. If כִּי is to be taken as giving a reason, it must be for their rejoicing in injustice. Otherwise כִּי must be taken as in v. 11. The people that Yahweh will raise up against Israel can be no other than the Assyrians (cf. 5.27). לָחַץ: 'oppress'; the plural is an *ad sensum* construction (Gr. § 145a–g). The attack of the

---

[1] Lodebar and Qarnaim are now identified with Umm ed-Dabar (or Dubar) (about fifteen kilometres south of Lake Gennesaret on the left bank of the Jordan) and with Sheikh Sa'd (approximately half-way between Damascus and Amman); see the *Westminster Historical Atlas*, London, ed. 2, 1947, Plates VIII and XVIII, and *Oxford Historical Atlas*, ed. H. G. May, Oxford 1962, p. 62, and in Gazetteer s.vv.

enemy will extend over the same area that is mentioned in 2 Kgs.
14.25 (see on v. 13), the only difference being that here the Brook
of the Arabah is mentioned instead of the Sea of Arabah. מִלְּבוֹא
חֲמָת means literally: 'from where one goes in to Hamath',
'from the entrance to Hamath'; by this is no doubt meant the
southern entrance to the valley between Lebanon and the Antilebanon. It has been thought that this is the place where the route
to North Syria began, and that it got its name from the best-
known city it passed. It must be remembered too that Hamath not
only was a city, but had territory which reached far to the south
(see on v. 2). The expression 'from the entrance to Hamath' is
therefore a regular expression for the northern frontier of Israel
(so also 2 Kgs. 14.25; 1 Kgs. 8.65; Num. 13.21; 34.8; Josh. 13.5;
Judg. 3.3, etc.). The brook of the Arabah is the southern frontier.
עֲרָבָה: 'steppe', 'plain'; with the article it is used especially of the
whole Jordan depression, including the Dead Sea and the region
south of it down to the Gulf of Akaba.[1] The Dead Sea is therefore called in the Old Testament among other names יָם הָעֲרָבָה
(Deut. 3.17; Josh. 3.16; 2 Kgs. 14.25). The brook of the Arabah
cannot be identified with certainty. The name shows that it
flowed out into the Jordan depression, probably into the Dead
Sea. Most think of the Wādi al-ahsā, which runs into the southern
end of the Dead Sea, and which in ancient times formed the
frontier between Moab and Edom. Others think that it would fit
better a river at the northern end of the Dead Sea, but are not
certain with which to identify it; the ʿen al-ġaraba east of Jericho
has been suggested. If a precise identification of the brook of the
Arabah cannot be made, we can establish that taken together the
expressions 'from the entrance to Hamath' and 'the brook of
the Arabah' signify the limits of the kingdom of Israel in the time
of Jeroboam II.[2]

---

[1] At the present day al-ʿaraba means the district south of the Dead Sea, while the
stretch between the Dead Sea and Lake Gennesaret is called al-ġōr 'the hole'.

[2] In Isa. 15.7 a נַחַל הָעֲרָבִים 'the river of the Euphrates poplar' occurs; in this
passage it also is a border river in Moab, but it is not known whether it is to the south or
the north. In the latter case it must be the frontier with Israel. The name is strikingly
similar to that of the brook in Amos. The LXX, which renders it by a plural χειμάρρου
τῶν δυσμῶν, read it as a plural, but misunderstood the word and connected it with עֶרֶב
'evening'. Wellhausen (p. 88) makes a quite inadmissible correction of the text to נַחַל
מִצְרַיִם, because elsewhere this is Israel's ideal southern frontier (1 Kgs. 8.65, 2 Chron.
7.8).

CHAPTER SEVEN

The third and last main division of the book of Amos is collected around five visions that the prophet had concerning the
fate of the people. The first two (7.1–3 and 4–6) describe a danger
threatening the people which is averted by the intercession of the
prophet. In the third and fourth visions (7.7–9 and 8.1–3), which
are also about the fate of the people, the intercession of the
prophet is lacking, from which we conclude that in them the disaster is immovably fixed. The fifth vision (9.1) is also not accompanied by any prayer by the prophet for the revocation of the
punishment, which is proclaimed as inevitable for the whole
people. From 9.11 onwards, however, the atmosphere changes
suddenly to promise of a bright future for the people. It has been
thought that the differing views of the final fate of the people are
due to the fact that they do not belong to the same period in the
life of the prophet. The two first, which count on Yahweh's for-
giveness, could belong to the time before his appearance proper,
when he was not fully convinced that the corruption of the people
was so great that it inevitably involved ruin for them. The other
visions accordingly will represent a more advanced recognition
by him of the state of affairs, after Yahweh had called him and
commanded him to proclaim disaster for the people. However,
the atmosphere changes again completely to one of promise from
9.11 on, and since the problem of threats and promises occurs in
other prophets too, and cannot be solved by the simple assumption of a difference in time and of development, this solution is
not a sufficient explanation in the case of Amos either. Nevertheless on other grounds we must assume that these visions extended
over a period of half a year. These visions are not simply a stylistic form, nor what we regard as hallucinations in the strict sense,
but have their origin in external phenomena, which are seen by
the prophet as something in which Yahweh makes known his
will. Connected with them he experiences in his mind Yahweh's
explanation of that which is seen (sublimated observations). We
should therefore picture the first vision as coming in the spring,
when the first brood of locusts is hatched out and causes destruction, in which the prophet sees the ruin of the people acted out.

The next is connected with the fires of the dry season, in the summer, the fourth with the picking of fruit in the autumn, and the fifth perhaps experienced at the autumn festival in the temple at Bethel, when the crowds of participants in the feast were gathered in and around the temple. The uniform nature of the visions is reminiscent of the collection of threats against the surrounding nations in chapters 1 and 2. It must have been created deliberately either by the prophet himself or by others after his expulsion from the Northern Kingdom.

Vv. 1–3: First vision: the locusts

V. 1. The prophet tells us by the phrase 'Thus the Lord God let me see' (cf. vv. 4, 7 and 8.1) that he feels that Yahweh is standing behind his experiences and has a purpose in them. What he experiences in his visions reflects Yahweh's intention for the people, and what Yahweh tells him to say he is bound to report to the people (see on 3.8). The MT reads 'and see [he] was in process of forming (part. יוֹצֵר) locusts', i.e. they were as it were formed directly in front of his eyes and swarmed forth. The subject of יוֹצֵר must be understood, but the context shows that it is Yahweh (cf. v. 4). On the verb יצר see on 4.13. גּוֹבַי sg. (only here and Nah. 3.17) is one of the many terms Hebrew has for 'locust' (see also Joel 1.4), and probably means the locust in the larva stage directly after hatching.[1] The derivation of the word is unknown. In place of יוֹצֵר some prefer to read יֵצֶר, in the sense of 'offspring' (cf. LXX ἐπιγονή). The word does not occur elsewhere in the Old Testament in this sense, but either with the meaning 'image' or the meaning 'thought'. לֶקֶשׁ is connected with the root לקשׁ 'to be late', from which מַלְקוֹשׁ 'the latter rain' comes (see on 4.7). It would fit the root meaning for לֶקֶשׁ to mean either the aftermath which grows after the haymaking (as does *leqshā* in Syriac), or the crop which is sustained by the latter rains in the spring. The first meaning fits best if the MT has been correctly transmitted in the rest of the verse, and if גִּזֵּי הַמֶּלֶךְ does

---

[1] See the pictures of the different stages of development of locusts in Driver's excursus on locusts in his commentary on Joel and Amos, ed. 2, pp. 83–93. According to others, however, the various words are names for different kinds of locusts.

not refer to the king's sheepshearing, as some assert, but to a privilege the king had of having the first grass of spring cut for his horses. The verb גזז is used specially of sheepshearing (Gen. 31.19; 38.12 f.) and the noun גֵּז of the shorn wool (Deut. 18.4; Job 31.20). גֵּז can, however, also be used of a field of grass that has been cut, or of the crop from it (Ps. 72.6). If this last meaning is chosen, the sense is that the land is attacked by a plague of locusts just as the grass had begun to grow again after the king had taken the best of the crop for his chariot-horses.[1] The plague therefore affected the population at large, who would not get food for their cattle until the rain fell again in the autumn. In place of the second לֶקֶשׁ the LXX has βροῦχος; this probably corresponds to the Hebrew יֶלֶק, which seems to mean the locust in the last stage of its development, before it can fly. The MT is preferable.

V. 2. וְהָיָה אִם כִּלָּה according to normal usage should be translated: 'and it shall happen, when they (i.e. the locusts, collective) have finished consuming'; but the imperfect consecutive fits very badly as a continuation here. It is therefore better to assume a corruption of the imperfect consecutive (וַיְהִי): 'and it happened, when they had finished' (אִם with perfect). It would be still better, however, both to read the imperfect consecutive, and also to redivide the consonantal text, so that it runs וַיְהִי הָא מְכַלֶּה: 'and when they were on the point of finishing . . ., I said'. עֵשֶׂב comprises not only grass, but all green plants (cf. Gen. 1.11). Amos intercedes for the people, and prays to Yahweh for mercy on the grounds that the people would not be able to endure because they are small, i.e. are poor, and ill-provided with resources, so that a catastrophe of this sort would mean their ruin. סלח 'forgive' (always with God as the subject). מִי is an accusative of circumstance: 'as to whom' = 'how' (cf. Gr. § 118m ff.).

V. 3. נָחַם (niphal) 'repent' (with עַל). זֹאת refers to the disaster which the locusts will bring upon the land. Yahweh promises that it will not come to anything. The passage shows us a picture of God which finds nothing offensive in the idea that Yahweh can

---

[1] Such a right is not attested with certainty in the Old Testament (not even in 1 Kgs. 18.5). On the other hand the Roman rulers of Syria later claimed this right in the month Nisan (see W. R. Smith, *Religion of the Semites*, ed. 3, London 1927, p. 246). It is in any case open to question whether it was the custom in ancient Israel to harvest the hay and to use it for feeding animals. The sense is perhaps that the king had the right wherever he went in the land of having the grass cut for his horses.

abandon a previous decision and give in to a man's prayers (cf. Gen. 18.22–33)).[1]

Vv. 4–6: The second vision: the all-consuming fire

V. 4. In the words קְרָא לָרִיב בָּאֵשׁ it is not רִיב that is to be connected with בָּאֵשׁ, since רִיב with בְּ means 'to bring a case against', but קְרָא: 'he called to the fire', and לָרִיב stands in the absolute: 'to judgement'. קָרָא with בְּ does not therefore have here its usual sense of 'call upon', but is almost the same as קָרָא with a direct object, 'to call'. A court scene unfolds, in which Yahweh is at the same time the prosecution, the judge and the one who carries out the sentence (similar court scenes are found in Isa. 3.13; Jer. 2.9; Hos. 4.1; Mic. 6.2). It is for this last purpose that fire is summoned. In summer, when everything is dry after months of strong sun, small fires start which spread in every direction with incredible speed, and burn up both grassland and trees (cf. Joel 1.19 f.). Firefighting operations are almost hopeless, since many streams and watercourses have dried up in summer. In the vision which Amos sees, even the great deep in which all springs have their origin is dried up by the strong heat. אֵשׁ, which is feminine, is the subject of the two following verbs. תְּהוֹם 'the primeval deep' (Gen. 1.2; 7.11) is always used without the article. Since the word itself is determinate, the accompanying adjective should really have had the article (Gr. § 126y). The perfect consecutive וְאָכְלָה expresses what will be the consequence of the drying up of the primeval deep. The next to be endangered would be הַחֵלֶק. This is understood by some in the sense of 'lot', 'portion', thinking of the whole land as the portion that was given the people by Yahweh. Others take the word in the sense of 'field' (cf. 2 Kgs. 9.10). The difference between the two senses is often so small that in practice they cannot be distinguished from one another. The meaning here is no doubt that by the time the primeval deep has been dried up everything will be so dry that the fire will consume the earth with all that is on it.

---

[1] In Ex. 10.18 f. Moses intercedes with Yahweh at the request of Pharaoh, and has the plague of locusts stopped. It happens through a violent west wind driving the locusts out over the Red Sea. Schneller reports that a strong cold west wind accompanied by rain can sometimes blow locusts away in a single night (*Kennst du das Land?*, rev. ed. Leipzig 1894, p. 140).

Vv. 5–6. Amos turns again to intercession, and Yahweh repents as in the first vision. In place of סְלַח־נָא we have חֲדַל־נָא 'cease, pray!'. On this understanding of the text, Amos' intercession comes before the catastrophe has been accomplished. The same was the case in the first vision, if we follow the suggested alteration of the text in v. 2.

Vv. 7–9: The third vision: the plumb line on the wall

V. 7. In contrast to the first two visions, Amos is here not a witness to the destruction or rather to that which would destroy the people as an entity, but witnesses a symbolic action which expresses the fall of the people, and this time the threat remains in force. He sees Yahweh standing over (נִצָּב עַל as in Gen. 28.13) a wall, which is described by the word אֲנָךְ. This literally means 'lead' (cf. the related languages), but here perhaps 'lead weight', 'plumb line'. If the sense of 'plumb line' is chosen, we must remember that a plumb line was not only used in the erection of walls to ensure that they were perpendicular, but also to test walls that were dilapidated and liable to be pulled down (cf. 2 Kgs. 21.13; Lam. 2.8; Isa. 28.17). It is rather artificial, however, to interpret 'a wall of a plumb line' as a wall which the test of a plumb line shows to be aslant, and which should therefore be pulled down. If we keep the meaning 'plumb line' for אֲנָךְ the word must be treated as a dittography the first time it appears (and the absolute חוֹמָה be read). It is from the lowering of the line (v. 8) and the threat in vv. 8 and 9 that it appears that the wall is ready to be pulled down. Others have interpreted אֲנָךְ as a tool that is used for demolition, 'crowbar' or the like; but in this case the word can hardly mean 'lead', which is a relatively soft metal, but rather 'steel' (cf. LXX ἀδάμας). But this meaning has no support in the related languages.[1] On this interpretation too the first אֲנָךְ must be deleted. Others again take חוֹמַת אֲנָךְ as a tough impenetrable wall (cf. the similes of the copper wall in Jer. 1.18, 15.20, and of the iron wall in Ezek. 4.3), and see this as a symbol of the irresistible power of the enemy (Assyria), which will plant itself immovably in the land. This interpretation, however, fits

---

[1] On the uses of lead see *BRL* s.v. 'Blei', cols. 111–13, and *IDB* s.v. Lead, vol. 3, pp. 103 f.

badly both the sense 'lead' and the fact that Yahweh stands on a wall with אֲנָךְ in his hand. Some try to overcome this difficulty by taking אֲנָךְ of the invincible weapon Yahweh has in his hands to undertake the devastation. It is not, however, usual to make weapons of lead. The most satisfactory solution is therefore still to keep the meaning 'plumb line' (and to delete the word on its first occurrence), and to understand the wall as a real wall, for instance the city wall.

V. 8. Talking with Amos Yahweh reveals that he will lower the plumb line in the midst of the people. Just as it can be established that a wall is dilapidated by lowering a plumb line alongside it, so it is a sign of the end of the people that Yahweh lowers a plumb line in their midst. But in spite of his plans to punish Israel, for Yahweh they will always remain his beloved and chosen people. עָבַר לְ 'pass by', i.e. 'spare'.

V. 9 shows in what the punishment will consist: the cult places will be laid waste, and the royal family exterminated. בָּמָה means literally simply a height,[1] but since the sanctuaries of the Canaanites were located on the high places about the country, the word comes to mean sacrificial high places, at which the Baal cult is observed. In their simplest form the sanctuaries on the high places were open-air sanctuaries. They had an altar, an unhewn stone or a carved stone pillar (מַצֵּבָה), a living tree or a wooden post (אֲשֵׁרָה). As time passed buildings were erected at the more popular holy places, and priests employed in them. At the time of the entry the Israelites took over the custom of worship at the high places from the Canaanites;[2] the difference was that they worshipped Yahweh in place of Baal, though of course under the strong influence of the Canaanite Baal cult. Our oldest sources find nothing objectionable in worship at the high places (see 1 Sam. 9.11 ff., cf. 1 Kgs. 3.4), but we can trace already in the Books of Kings the later condemnation of this worship. This is evident from, for instance, the report of Jeroboam I's erection of sacrificial houses on the high places, together with the appointment of a non-legitimate priesthood (1 Kgs. 12.31 ff.). According

---

[1] According to Albright the *bāmāh* was originally a burial mound with a cult of the departed, but later accompanied by a fertility cult ('The High Place in Ancient Palestine', *Volume du Congrès Strasbourg 1956*, SVT IV, Leiden 1957, pp. 242-58).

[2] Worship at high places is found also among the Moabites, see the Mesha stone *NSI*, p. 1, *KAI*, No. 181, l. 3, and also Isa. 15.2, 16.12.

to the Books of Kings worship on the high places was forbidden in Josiah's reformation (2 Kgs. 23.5 ff.), and this has left its mark on the picture they give of the history. The same viewpoint is also expressed in Deuteronomy (see 12.1 ff.). This strong hostility is based on the harmful effect on Israel of the worship at the high places. Some of the first to realize this and to oppose it were the prophets. In Amos' proclamation the attack on the worship of the high places does not have a prominent place; his opposition to it is a natural consequence of his condemnation of the corrupt nature of the cultus in general. יִשְׂחָק as a name for the people is found only here and in v. 16. It is usually spelt יִצְחָק. The name is paralleled by Amos' use elsewhere of another of the ancestors of the nation, Jacob, to refer to Israel; he is only thinking here in fact of the people of the Northern Kingdom, as appears from the end of the verse, which is directed against 'the house of Jeroboam'. By this is meant not primarily the king's family (his wives and children), but the dynasty, which is to be exterminated (compare Hosea's threat against the house of Jehu, 1.4). Amos pictures the extermination as being at the hands of an enemy power, i.e. the Assyrians, cf. 6.14.

Vv. 10–17: The clash with the high-priest at Bethel

The series of visions is interrupted here by a narrative in prose (apart from the prophecies in vv. 11 and 17), of a conflict between Amos and Amaziah, the high-priest in Bethel. In indignation at Amos' preaching, Amaziah lodged a complaint with king Jeroboam, in which he accused Amos of conspiring against the king, and taking part in activities injurious to the state. Jeroboam's answer is not reported, but Amaziah himself forbids Amos to prophesy in the Northern Kingdom, and orders him out, as being a professional prophet who had appeared there for the sake of gain. Amos rejects this accusation, and directs a powerful threat against Amaziah and his family. The passage ends abruptly, without a report of Amos' subsequent fate. Since, however, it is hardly probable that he continued his prophetic activity in the Northern Kingdom after this clash, vv. 10–17 should really be placed at the end of the book if the order of the individual passages were chronological. The reason for the redactor placing

8—B.A.

this report here is no doubt the presence of the threat against the house of Jeroboam in v. 9, so that we have here a typical example of the catchword principle.

There is no reason to deny the authenticity of this report. The circumstance that it is in prose, in contrast to the rest of the book, is not peculiar, since a report of the conflict between Amos and Amaziah would most naturally be given in prose. There is no convincing objection to the idea that the narrative may in the main be given in Amos' own words (transferred to the third person), whether we take the view that it was written down (like the rest of the book) by himself after his return to Judah, or by his followers.

V. 10. A sanctuary as large as that of Bethel (see on 3.14) had of course a very large number of priests. 'The priest of Bethel' must therefore mean the high-priest of the whole sanctuary. From the meaning of the priest's name ('Yahweh is strong') it can be concluded that he was a Yahweh worshipper, since it is unthinkable that a man whose name is compounded with Yahweh could have been put in charge of the sanctuary of another God. We can therefore be sure that Yahweh was officially worshipped at Bethel, even if the form of cultus which was practised there was far from satisfying the stricter prophets of Yahweh. For prophets of the type of Amos and Hosea it was only a disguised form of Baal cult.

The sanctuary in Bethel was especially closely connected with the royal house because of Jeroboam I's provisions for this sanctuary after the division of the country (1 Kgs. 12), so that in contrast to many smaller sanctuaries it was a state sanctuary (v. 13). Amaziah therefore feels himself obliged to lodge a complaint with the king, when he finds that Amos' preaching is directed against the king. The king is Jeroboam II, who resided in the capital Samaria. The report made is that Amos has 'made a conspiracy' against the king. The verb קָשַׁר (literally 'to bind') can be used of a treasonable conspiracy (e.g. that of Zimri against Elah, 1 Kgs. 16.16, and that of the court officials against Joash, 2 Kgs. 12.21). In view of the fact that prophets lay behind the division of the kingdom after the death of Solomon (1 Kgs. 11.29–39), and behind Jehu's revolution (1 Kgs. 19.15–18 and 2 Kgs. 9.1–10), it is not unjustified to consider the possibility that Amos may have had plans to remove the king. But the idea must be rejected. We do not elsewhere get the impression that his preaching was

directed against the king; it is only in 7.9 that threats against the
king himself are found, and it is noteworthy that this is not an
ambiguous hint that he will be killed in an insurrection, but contains the clear idea (as elsewhere in the book) that the punishment
will be carried out by the hostile power whom Yahweh will use
as his instrument. His 'conspiring' therefore consists simply in
his prophecy of the king's death, while he has not urged any
action to hasten it on. But even this according to the ideas of the
time would be enough to do harm to the position of the king. The
prophecy of the fall of the dynasty is to be understood not just as
an insult to the king, to the length of whose reign it would make
no difference, but as being a dangerous proceeding, because a
word uttered with power is also able to perform what it declares.
A king cannot be indifferent to the blessings or curses of others,
because he does not know how much power there is in the word.

The hiphil of כול can be used of a measure which cannot contain all that is put into it; this image also fits the land, which cannot contain all the words of the prophet. But the verb can also be
used in the sense of 'endure', 'bear'; and this gives an equally
good sense, the thought being of the harm caused by both the
quantity (כְּל־) and the content of the words.

V. 11. Amaziah's report of Amos' preaching is basically correct. Amaziah limits his words to 'Jeroboam shall die by the
sword', while the threat in v. 9 referred to the house of Jeroboam,
that is the whole dynasty; but Amos hardly meant by this expression that Jeroboam himself should escape scot-free, so that Amaziah is right in understanding the threat as if it were directed at the
king himself too. It is a separate point that the fulfilment of the
prophecy corresponded better to the language of v. 9 than to that
of v. 11, since Jeroboam was not himself overthrown; but his
family remained in power only a few years after his death. The
threat of the deportation of the people corresponds to Amos'
utterances on other occasions (see 5.27 and 6.7).

V. 12. The silence of the account about the king's reaction to
Amaziah's report cannot be interpreted as meaning that he took
no notice of the matter, or that Amaziah in his eagerness did not
wait for the king's answer, so that he is acting on his own account
when he expels Amos. The expulsion must certainly be interpreted as having the king's authority behind it. Amos must be
said to have escaped lightly in comparison with the treatment of

Uriah and Jeremiah in Judah under king Jehoiakim (see Jer. 26.20–24).

Amaziah addresses Amos by the title חֹזֶה 'seer', which has the same meaning as רֹאֶה. For the two verbs see on 1.1. It appears from the inserted note at 1 Sam. 9.9 that the 'seer' (רֹאֶה) is the same as was later called the 'prophet' נָבִיא (cf. on 2.11 and 3.7). Amaziah also uses the corresponding verb of Amos' activity (in the niphal); it appears from this, and from Amos' protest at being classed together with the *nabis*, that חֹזֶה and נָבִיא are used here with no difference in sense. The word חֹזֶה is clearly used here with a disparaging note in reference to Amos' visions, which he must have adduced in his utterances (cf. 7.1 ff.). Amaziah treats Amos as one of the professional fortune-tellers, who sold their knowledge for money, and told people what they wanted to hear (see Mic. 3.5, 11). In ancient times it was the custom for men to pay seers when they went to ask advice from them, for instance about runaway asses (1 Sam. 9.7 f.). The worse sort of seer made money out of people's eagerness to be told something good or fortunate, and preached peace even when disaster threatened the people (cf. Jer. 6.14; 23.16 f.; 28.1 ff.). Some of the seers or *nabis* did in fact belong to bands into which men were taken to learn the art of prophesying as a way of making a living. The individual members of the band were called בֶּן־נָבִיא, cf. 'the sons of the prophets' in 1 Kgs. 20.35; 2 Kgs. 2.3,5,15; 4.1, etc. Amaziah treated Amos as a professional prophet of this sort, and told him to take himself home to Judah, and make his living there by his work as a prophet. The high-priest, as a man of high rank, must have looked down on Amos, whose clothing would have revealed his lowly status. Amaziah was not ashamed therefore to use any means to taunt him. Perhaps he also hints that he will have opportunities of good income in his own country, if it is part of his programme to proclaim the fall of the Northern Kingdom. בְּרַח־לְךָ 'take yourself off' (לְךָ ethical dative). אכל לחם 'eat bread' = 'make one's living'.

V. 13. Amos' preaching has in any case had so bad an effect that Amaziah does not wish him to appear in Bethel (בֵּית־אֵל accusative of place, Gr. § 118d–g). One cannot but hear in the reason he gives for this his pride at being priest at the famous sanctuary, especially because it comes under the king (מִקְדַּשׁ־מֶלֶךְ). He further describes it as בֵּית־מַמְלָכָה 'the temple of the kingdom', i.e. it does not belong to a single man or city, but to the whole kingdom.

V. 14. Amos begins his answer by rejecting the accusation that he is a professional prophet.[1] בֶּן־נָבִיא does not mean 'son of a prophet', but 'member of a prophetic band' (cf. above). It cannot be concluded from this repudiation that Amos looked down on all prophets. On the contrary it appears from passages like 2.11 f. and 3.7 that Yahweh uses prophets to proclaim his will, and they must necessarily do this when Yahweh reveals himself to them. Amos only wishes to protest at being included in the same class as the professional prophets, whose preaching was not dictated by Yahweh, but by the wish to earn money. This is why he points out that he has another profession, which he only left because Yahweh had laid upon him a quite specific task.[2] כִּי here: 'but'. בּוֹקֵר must mean 'one who herds cattle' (בָּקָר). If the text is correct, we are told here that Amos herded both cattle and sheep. On the other hand the word occurs nowhere else in Hebrew, and there are strong objections to the correctness of the text. One point is that Amos continues in v. 15 by saying that Yahweh took him from the flock הַצֹּאן, and another that the LXX renders בּוֹקֵר by αἰπόλος 'goatherd'. So בּוֹקֵר is probably a corruption of נוֹקֵד, which is used in Amos 1.1; a confusion of נ with ב and of ד with ר is easily conceivable. Apart from his occupation as a shepherd he made his living by dressing sycamore trees. The verb בלס occurs only here in the Old Testament; the meaning is fairly cer-

---

[1] On this interpretation the correct translation is 'I am no prophet'. The English Revised Version has 'I was no prophet'. This translation is supported by H. H. Rowley ('Was Amos a Nabi?', *Festschrift Otto Eissfeldt*, Halle 1947, pp. 191–8), I. Engnell ('Profetismens Ursprung och Uppkomst', *RoB* 8, 1949, p. 16) and A. S. Kapelrud (*Central Ideas in Amos*, Oslo 1956, p. 7). It is Rowley who has given the fullest argument for this interpretation. He describes Amos' indignant reply to Amaziah as follows: 'It is not money I prophesy for. I am a prophet by divine constraint. I had not chosen the calling of a prophet, or trained to be a prophet. God laid his hand upon me, and charged me with his word, and I had delivered it where he constrained me to deliver it' (op. cit., p. 198). The difference of view between Rowley and myself turns in the last instance upon whether Amos has used the word prophet (*nabi*, and the verb derived from it) in two different senses. It cannot be denied that Micah 3.5, 11 and Jeremiah 23.9–40 use the word for a group of men from which these two prophets dissociate themselves; compare also the description of the false prophets in 1 Kgs. 22. I do not want therefore to deny that Amos felt himself to be a prophet, and asserted that he was speaking the word of Yahweh, but claim that in his speech to Amaziah he dissociates himself from being a prophet (*nabi*) in a depreciatory sense.

[2] It also appears from Amos' words that he cannot have belonged to the so-called 'cult-prophets' (see on 2.11). Isaiah on the other hand to all appearances did belong to the *nabis*.

tain, since *balas* in Arabic and Ethiopic means 'fig', so that the corresponding verb must mean 'to handle figs' or 'to raise figs'. The following noun declares more specifically that these were the fruit of the sycamore tree (שִׁקְמָה*, plural שִׁקְמִים 'sycamore tree'). They are not regarded as so good or so tasty as figs proper; the fruit is rather bitter, but by making an incision in them before they are ripe, one can make some of the juice run out. The rest then ferments, and gives the fruit a sweet taste, which is reminiscent of figs proper. It is certainly this treatment that LXX had in mind with its translation κνίζων συκάμινα 'who makes incisions in sycamore figs'.[1] Tekoa lies too high to be able to grow sycamore berries. They were, however, common down on the coastal plain, and can also be cultivated in the warm Jordan valley, and in the fertile oases by the Dead Sea. This does not make it impossible that Amos should have supported himself as a sideline by growing sycamores at one of these places, which are near enough to Tekoa for this to be combined with his work as a shepherd. He was probably able to drive his herds with him when he went to attend to his sycamore trees.

V. 15. He only interrupted his work as a shepherd because Yahweh took him away from the flock and told him to go to the Northern Kingdom to preach against the people there. מאחרי literally 'from being behind' (cf. of David 2 Sam. 7.8 and Ps. 78.70 f.). אֶל has the same significance here as עַל 'against', cf. v. 16. In spite of the sinfulness of the Northern Kingdom Yahweh in speaking of it had to recognize it as his people.

V. 16. Having thus reprimanded Amaziah Amos goes on to declare to him how Yahweh will punish him because he has forbidden Amos to proclaim Yahweh's word in the Northern Kingdom (note the contrast between 'You say' in v. 16 and 'Yahweh says' in v. 17). נטף hiphil (1) 'let drip' (9.13), (2) 'prophesy,' 'preach' as here (cf. Mic. 2.6, 11).[2] Isaac is a name for the Northern Kingdom as in v. 9.

V. 17. Amaziah's family must by contemporary ideas suffer together with him. His wife will be disgraced by being reduced to

---

[1] Some, however, hold that the reference is to the infestation of the fruit with insects, which must be removed before it is fit to eat.

[2] Many maintain that the verb is used contemptuously, in that the reference is to spittle pouring from the mouth of an ecstatic prophet; but the verb can also be used in a transferred sense of the stream of speech.

a harlot's existence in the same city where she has been until now one of the most distinguished women. The thought is not as some have suggested that soldiers will ravish her after the conquest of the city (Isa. 13.16 and Zech. 14.2 use for this the verb שׁגל). She will lose her means of support, and will therefore be compelled to make her living by prostitution. The addition 'in the city' would also be pointless if the thought were of her being violated by force. The enemy will cut down Amaziah's children, and divide up their property. The idea may be that the Assyrian kings let their own subjects settle in conquered territories and get land there. A man as highly placed as the chief-priest of Bethel must certainly have had a large estate. The worst fate, however, will befall Amaziah himself; the former high-priest will suffer the indignity of having to eat unclean food for the rest of his life in a foreign land. In the thought of the time Yahweh reigns only in his own land, while men must worship other gods when they journey to foreign lands (1 Sam. 26.19). They can then no longer bring Yahweh the sacrifices which are necessary to hallow the crops, with the consequence that all foods eaten are unclean (see Hos. 9.3 f.). Finally Amos repeats the threat of the deportation of the whole people, the same threat that Amaziah had spoken of in his report to the king (v. 11). The narrative ends abruptly without telling anything of the effect of Amos' words on Amaziah, or whether Amos complied with the expulsion order. Probably Amos appeared no more as a prophet in the Northern Kingdom, but returned to his home country.

CHAPTER EIGHT

Vv. 1–3: The fourth vision: the basket of summer fruit

After the report of 7.10–17 breaks off, the book continues with a description of a vision which in content is related to the three visions in 7.1–9, and particularly with the last of them, vv. 7ff. As in that vision Amos sees something that is a symbol of the punishment, but does not actually witness the punishment being carried out; it is common to them both that the punishment announced is not taken back as a result of the intercession of the prophet.

V. 1. The vision is introduced with the same phrase as in 7.1 and 4. A basket (כְּלוּב) with ripe fruits is the external occasion of the vision. קַיִץ literally 'heat', 'summer' (Gen. 8.22) means here 'summer fruit' (cf. 2 Sam. 16.1).

V. 2. In a conversation with the prophet Yahweh himself interprets the vision (cf. 7.8). The reported conversation between Yahweh and the prophet does not necessarily show that the vision is more than a 'sublimated observation'. The conversation could in fact be a reflection of the prophet's meditations on the vision and his recognition of Yahweh's will in what he experienced. The ripe fruits will not be the occasion for the merriment and song of the Autumn Festival; on the contrary they lead to the thought that the people are ripe for disaster (קֵץ) because of their sins, so that they give warning of mourning and lamentation. Inasmuch as the summer-fruits point forward to the end of the year, there is a factual connection between the two words קַיִץ and קֵץ, which are also reminiscent of one another in sound, although etymologically they have no connection.[1] In the Book of Daniel the idea of the קֵץ has an important place; in this, however, the 'time of the end' not only brings judgement to the apostates, but contains hope for the pious, who have suffered for their faith (see Dan. 8.17, 19; 9.26; 11.27; 12.4, 6, 13). אֶל means the same as עַל, as in 7.15. The result of the vision is the same as in 7.8 (end).

V. 3 describes what the punishment consists in. The mourning and lamentation that are announced are contrasted to the rejoicing of the people at the Autumn Festival. שִׁירוֹת 'songs' fits badly as a subject to הֵילִילוּ 'lament': since furthermore שִׁירִים is the normal form of the plural, the text is improved by vocalizing שָׁרוֹת 'female singers'. It is difficult to decide if הֵיכָל here is the temple or the palace, since female singers probably performed in both places at the feasts. The original consonantal text would also permit the vocalization שָׂרוֹת 'princesses'.[2] 'On that day' must in this context refer to the day of punishment; it is a regular eschato-

---

[1] קַיִץ corresponds to the Arabic qaiẓ and the Aramaic qaiṭa, while קֵץ is related to קצץ 'cut off', cf. Arabic qaṣṣa and Aramaic kṣṣ. A similar connection between the harvest and the day of judgement is found in Matt. 13.39; the harvest is the end of the world. An example of how an external phenomenon can give rise to a play on words is also found in Jer. 1.11 f., where an almond tree (שָׁקֵד) makes the prophet think that Yahweh is vigilant (שֹׁקֵד) over his word to fulfil it.

[2] The translation of the LXX φατνώματα (coffers in a ceiling) corresponds to Hebrew קֹרוֹת (beams, rafters), but this gives no intelligible sense here.

logical term (see also vv. 9, 13 and 9.11). The cause of the mourning is the many dead, whose bodies are left lying on all the roads, with no one to bury them. The brevity of the text does not allow us to decide whether they have died at the hand of the enemy or through pestilence. The similarity with 6.10 could argue for this latter alternative; there too the word הָס 'silence!' is found. It is probably to be understood in both passages as a warning not to mention the name of Yahweh in so serious a situation. הָס cannot be taken as an adverb ('they shall be cast out in silence'), but only as an interjection. In place of הִשְׁלִיךְ 'one throws out' we could read הָשְׁלַךְ 'there are thrown out', so that רֹב הַפֶּגֶר 'the number of bodies' becomes the subject, ignoring the accents to do this (MT reads literally: 'the dead bodies are many! in every place one throws out, silence!').

Vv. 4–14: A collection of threats and oracles of judgement

The first section vv. 4–8 is directed against those who deal dishonestly (this means here the landowners, who controlled the corn trade) and in form and in tone is reminiscent of the oracles of punishment in chapters 3–6. Vv. 4 and 6 show an especial similarity to 2.6 and 7 (see further the commentary on them). The passage has no close link with the preceding one.

V. 4. 'Hear this!' refers to what follows (cf. 3.1; 4.1 and 5.1: 'Hear this word'). The verb שָׁאַף, literally 'persecute', can be taken in the first half-verse as having the same sense as שׁוּף 'crush', cf. 2.7, where the prophet protests against injustice to the דַּלִּים and עֲנָוִים in a similar manner to that found here of the אֶבְיוֹן and עֲנִיֵּי־אָרֶץ; the latter can be derived either with the kethibh from עָנָו or with the qere from עָנִי. Both words are used without much perceptible difference of those who are the worst placed in the social system. וְלַשְׁבִּית 'and to make to cease' (hiphil infinitive = וּלְהַשְׁבִּית Gr. § 53q) makes a break in the construction, unless the participle is understood from v. 4a in the sense of 'that are eager for'. The text of the LXX καὶ καταδυναστεύοντες is taken by many as evidence that v. 4b also contained a participle (כֹּבְשִׁים or עֹשְׁקִים); but this is not justified, for the LXX often skims over a difficult text and contents itself with giving the general sense. MT should therefore be retained, in spite of the difficult construction. To 'make them to cease' means to destroy them by heavy-handed and shameless treatment. What this consists in is told in the next verse.

V. 5. The traders felt the new moon feasts and sabbaths to be a drag on their trade. The passage is evidence that at this period the day of the new moon and the sabbath were kept holy among other things by a cessation of all trade. We do not gather Amos' own view of this custom from the castigation he directs at the corndealers; although elsewhere he directs hard words at the feasts and cult of the people, in this context he only wishes to impress on them that while otherwise they lay undue weight on the feasts, when they get in the way of the exploitation of the poor, they regard them as a nuisance. We have further confirmation of the celebration of these two feast-days under the monarchy also in Isa. 1.13 f.; Hos. 2.13 and 2 Kgs. 4.23. In this last passage the father of the dead boy says to his wife when she wants to send a message to the prophet Elisha: 'Why will you go to him today? It is neither new moon nor sabbath!' It is evident from this that it was the established custom to visit the prophets on these days. The day of the new moon on its own is attested as a feast-day already in the time of Saul (1 Sam. 20.5, 24). Other passages in the Old Testament treat the sabbath and the day of the new moon as much older than the period of the monarchy. The Decalogue (Ex. 20.8 and Deut. 5.14) has the sabbath commandment given on Sinai, and the first account of creation takes the holiness of the seventh day right back to the creation of the world (Gen. 2.3). According to Lev. 23.23–25; Num. 10.10; 28.11 f., the feast of the new moon was also ordained by Moses. It is not in itself impossible that the Israelites already celebrated certain feasts connected with the moon in the wilderness period apart from the day of the new moon, and that this usage has left its traces in the laws. The sabbath would in that case have originally been the day of the full moon. It is usually assumed, however, that both the word sabbath and the practice of keeping holy the seventh day are of Babylonian origin, and that the Israelites first took over the custom after the entry into Canaan, where it had been introduced under Babylonian influence. The Hebrew word שַׁבָּת 'sabbath' is not formed from the verb שבת 'rest'. The verb is derived from the substantive, which in turn comes from the Babylonian *šabattu*, a word whose etymology is not certain.[1] It is used of the day of the full moon, that is the fourteenth day of the month. It is very probable that apart from the day of the full moon, the other changes of the moon were also celebrated in Babylonia (the 7th, 21st and 28th of the month). In any case they were regarded as less lucky days ('*dies nefasti*'), on which the king as high-priest must not offer sacrifice to the gods. Even if the Hebrew sabbath was originally a day of the changes of the moon, as in Babylonia (cf. the mention of it together with the day of the new moon here and in Isa. 1.13 f., Hos. 2.13 and 2 Kgs. 4.23), it changed its character in Israel, and became independent of the changes of the moon, with a fixed place in the week; nor was it an unlucky day, but a day of rest and a feast-day.[2]

'To open the corn' means to open the stores of corn to sell it. With לְהַקְטִין we have again the prophet's own words. The corn-dealers sell on the principle, 'short measure, top prices', and they use false weights too if they can get away with it. אֵיפָה is a measure of capacity (e.g. of corn or of liquids), and is approximately 39·3 litres, the same as a bath, or one tenth of a homer.[3] שֶׁקֶל 'shekel' (literally 'weight', cf. the verb שָׁקַל 'to weigh', Gen. 23.16) is the normal unit of weight.

The shekel is divided into פִּים, ⅔ shekel, בֶּקַע ½ shekel, רֶבַע ¼ shekel and גֵּרָה 'a grain', 1/20 shekel. The larger weights are the talent (כִּכָּר) and the mina (מָנֶה). On the Babylonian system a talent was sixty minas, and a mina was sixty shekels, so that there were 3,600 shekels in a talent; but in Palestine and Syria another system was also known, in which a talent is sixty minas, but a mina is only fifty shekels (see Exod. 38.25 ff.; Ezek. 45.12, where the text should be corrected to read fifty and not five shekels). On the situation in

---

[1] According to some it is the day when the gods are 'calmed', i.e. a sort of day of atonement; according to others it is the day when the moon 'is finished', or full-grown, that is the day of the full moon; others again derive it from the verb 'to judge' (=Hebrew שפט), that is, a day for legal proceedings.

[2] On this question see further H. Gunkel, *Genesis*, Göttingen, ed. 3, 1910, pp. 115 f. (on Gen. 2.3), B. Meissner, *Babylonien und Assyrien*, vol. 2 (Kulturgeschichtliche Bibliothek I:4), Heidelberg 1925, pp. 92 f., and H. Ringgren, *Israelite Religion*, London 1966, pp. 200–2.

[3] See *BRL* s.v. 'Masse', cols. 366–8, *IDB* s.v. Weights and Measures, vol. 4, pp. 834 ff. Benzinger (*Hebräische Archäologie*, ed. 3, Leipzig 1927, p. 194) calculates the ephah as 36·44 litres.

Ras Shamra see F. Thureau-Dangin, 'Un Comptoir de Laine Pourpre à Ugarit', *Syria* 15, 1934, pp. 137–46. On the Babylonian standard a talent was 60·6 kilograms, and a shekel accordingly about 16 grams, but weights of this size have up to now not been found in Palestine. On the other hand a weight has been found with the inscription פִּים (cf. 1 Sam. 13.21), weighing about 7·45 grams. Since a פִּים is ⅔ of a shekel, this would give a shekel of 11·17 grams. For confirmation we have other weights without inscription which are of roughly this weight, and clearly are a shekel (see *BRL* s.v. 'Gewicht', cols. 185–8, *IDB* s.v. Weights and Measures, vol. 4, pp. 828 ff.). The value of a shekel varies of course according to the metal it is made of. There were considerable difficulties in the calculation of the relationship of silver shekels to gold shekels, since the relation between the value of the two metals is one of 1:13½ (see Benzinger, *Hebräische Archäologie*, ed. 3, Leipzig 1927, pp. 197 ff.). A calculation of the value of a shekel in our money gives a false picture, because its purchasing power was quite different from what it would be now; for example for two silver shekels a man could buy a ram or 36 litres of wheat or 72 litres of barley (see Lev. 5.15; 2 Kgs. 7.16).

At the time of Amos minted money was quite unknown (it was introduced first by the Persians), but metal bars, rings, etc. were weighed and the value calculated according to the metal they were made of. When the corndealers sold corn to the poor, they demanded larger quantities of metal than was fair for corn, which was in any case given in short measure. עוּת piel 'bend', 'curve'. The word could also be read עָוֵּת from עוה piel 'twist', 'distort', of which עוּת is a by-form. To 'bend the balances of falsehood', is a way of saying 'to weigh falsely'; this is strongly condemned in the laws (see Deut. 25.13 ff.; Lev. 19.35 f., cf. Ezek. 45.10 f.; Prov. 20.10 and Hos. 12.8).

V. 6 must in this context mean that the traders push the corn prices so high that the poor have at last to sell themselves as slaves, when they can no longer find the money (cf. Lev. 25.39). The rich can then buy them for a trifle (cf. 2.6, where the expression 'sell for silver and a pair of sandals' also occurs). The last three words of the verse, which are spoken by the traders, are undeniably difficult as a continuation of their words from v. 5a after the insertion of the prophet's words in v. 5b and 6a. This has

naturally led the commentators to delete the words. The sense is
that the rich are so mean as to sell to the poorest people the lowest
quality of corn, and make them pay through the nose for it. מַפָּל
(from נפל) 'refuse'.

V. 7. While vv. 4–6 contain the words of the prophet against
the rich and his report of what they themselves say, in this verse
he has Yahweh underline with an oath that he will not leave their
treatment of the poor unpunished. He swears by גְּאוֹן יַעֲקֹב 'the
pride of Jacob', which here does not mean Jacob's conceited
boasting (as in 6.8), but that of which Jacob is proud, that is,
Yahweh; so that the expression corresponds to בְּנַפְשׁוֹ 6.8 and בְּקָדְשׁוֹ
4.2.[1] But it is certainly not accidental that Amos here calls Yahweh 'the pride of Jacob', since he wants to remind the people
what Yahweh ought to be to them. אִם in an oath means 'not' (Gr.
§ 149).

V. 8. The punishment is an earthquake, which is compared
with the rise and fall of the Nile. The verse, or perhaps the first
half-verse, takes the form of a question ('Shall not . . . because of
this . . .?'), expecting the answer yes. זֹאת refers back to vv. 4 ff.
The verb רגז 'be agitated' is here used of the movement of the
earth caused by the earthquake, cf. 1 Sam. 14.15. The tremors
will be so violent that the earth will rise and sink like the waters
of the Nile. The comparison is not entirely felicitous, since the
Nile rises and falls gradually, and is of benefit to the land. The
probable explanation is that Amos had never been in Egypt, and
only knew of the rise of the Nile by hearsay. In the MT the rise is
compared first with the light (כָּאוֹר), i.e. with the sunrise, but in
place of this most commentators correctly prefer 'like the Nile'
(כַּיְאוֹר), since the consonant י could easily be lost (cf. also 9.5 and
כִּיאוֹר מִצְרַיִם in the parallel line). יְאוֹר 'river' is used particularly of
the Nile. גרש niphal, literally 'be driven out', here of the waters
which are forced out of their usual courses (cf. Isa. 57.20 and in
Ras Shamra 2(III AB) IV, 12). שקע qal and niphal 'sink'. The
reading of the kethib נשקה is undoubtedly an error (cf. 9.5), since
the niphal of שקה 'drink' makes no sense here, and in any case the
verb does not occur anywhere else in the Old Testament in the
niphal.

---

[1] In Jer. 2.11 and Ps. 106.20 the word כָּבוֹד is similarly used as a periphrasis for Yahweh.

Vv. 9–10: The day of judgement will come with darkness and mourning

V. 9. 'On that day' refers to the day of judgement (cf. v. 3). A sudden darkening of the sun at midday will paralyse people with fear. Eclipses were often regarded by people of this period as warnings of disasters. It has been calculated that eclipses of the sun took place on 9th February 784 B.C. and on 15th June 763 B.C. Amos may perhaps have had a clear recollection of the uncanny atmosphere and panic that they created, and used them as his starting-point in his description of the day of judgement. Signs in the heavenly bodies occur also in the descriptions of the day of judgement in several other of the prophetic books (Isa. 13.10; Joel 2.10; 3.4; 4.15, cf. Matt. 24.29, etc.).

V. 10. The cheerful atmosphere at the pilgrimage festivals (חָג, see 5.21) will change to mourning, and the songs of joy will be replaced by lamentation (קִינָה, see 5.1); for the thought cf. Hos. 2.13. It was customary as a sign of mourning to put on clothing of coarse hairy material (שַׂק), which was wrapped around the loins (מָתְנַיִם), and to pull out one's hair (cf. 2 Sam. 3.31; Ezek. 7.18; Isa. 15.2 f.; Jer. 48.37).[1] The baldness referred to is therefore not a natural baldness, but the result of pulling hair out as a sign of mourning. The custom is alluded to in Deut. 14.1. The mourning which will come upon them is compared with the bitterest form of mourning of all, mourning for an only son (יָחִיד). The loss of an only son or daughter was felt even more bitterly then than it is in our time, since men felt themselves much more strongly members of a family which should be carried on through offspring, preferably through a son. Compare with this passage Jer. 6.26; Zech. 12.10. The suffixes in וְשַׂמְתִּיהָ and וְאַחֲרִיתָהּ are neuter (Gr. § 122g): 'it' is the grievous event which will come. The end of it will not be a cessation of mourning. Rather they have a permanent prospect of mourning. The thought could be expressed in other words as that they would have mourning from start till finish. יוֹם מַר 'a bitter day', i.e. a day that brings sorrow and distress.

---

[1] On the Ahiram sarcophagus women can be seen with sackcloth on their loins and naked down to their waists (*AOB*, illus. 665, *ANEP* 459).

Vv. 11–12: They will be punished with hunger and thirst for the word of Yahweh

V. 11 is introduced with the same phrase as came in 4.2. We no longer hear now of a single day of distress as at the beginning of v. 9, but the distress is said to extend over a longer period of time. The single day of v. 9 should in any case not be taken literally, but is simply to be understood as the day which is the prelude to the disasters. When hunger is mentioned one thinks inevitably of bodily hunger, just as thirst in v. 12a is bodily thirst which will afflict the people as punishment; but in vv. 11b and 12b it is emphasized that both are a spiritual privation, of hearing the word of Yahweh. This is interpreted as meaning that Yahweh will keep silent because he is angry (cf. 1 Sam. 14.37), and therefore the people long for a word from him (perhaps through a prophet), which will tell them that now the distress will cease. But this interpretation is artificial. Both vv. 11b and 12b express rather that there is a hunger and a thirst which are far worse than bodily hunger and thirst, and that the people will at length repent and come to their senses, so that they long to hear Yahweh's words again. The passage therefore contains a thought similar to that of Deut. 8.3 ('man does not live by bread alone, but man lives by everything that proceeds out of the mouth of the Lord', cf. in the New Testament John 4.34). If this is the case, both vv. 11b and 12b are probably added comments, which perhaps were first written in the margin, and later inserted into the actual text by mistake.

V. 12. נוע is used in the same way as in 4.8, where the thought is clearly of physical thirst. 'From sea to sea' means from the Mediterranean to the Dead Sea. They represent the western and southern frontiers of the land (cf. 2 Kgs. 14.25, and the Brook of the Arabah in 6.14), while צָפוֹן and מִזְרָח are the northern and eastern frontiers. מִזְרָח 'sunrise', 'east'. שׁוּט: qal and polel 'wander'. The end of the verse insists that their efforts will be in vain.

Vv. 13–14: Punishment for those who worship Yahweh in the wrong way

If these two verses are not originally a separate utterance, but are connected to what precedes them, v. 13 underlines the correctness of the view that the thirst of vv. 11–12 was originally physical thirst, which has now become so great that even young girls and men, who should have the greatest powers of resistance, will faint. 'In that day' is used in the same way as in v. 9. עלף in the hithpael (1) 'wrap oneself up' Gen. 38.14 (2) 'faint' Jon. 4.8 and here, cf. the pual in Isa. 51.20.[1] The verb is governed by הַבְּתוּלוֹת and not by הַבַּחוּרִים, because it stands before the first of these two words.

V. 14 gives the motivation for the prediction of punishment. To swear by a god means the same as to honour and worship him (cf. Deut. 6.13 and 10.20, which insist that Israel shall swear by Yahweh, see also Jer. 4.2, 5.7, 12.16, Zeph. 1.5, Isa. 48.1). The verse contains three different oath formulas, which probably each contain a reference to the god of a local sanctuary. The second expression, 'as thy god lives, O Dan', alludes to the worship of Yahweh in the form of a bull image of gold in Dan (cf. 1 Kgs. 12.29 and Judg. 18.30). The oath formula corresponds to חַי־יְהוָה 'as the Lord lives' (1 Sam. 14.39). This reference to the image of Yahweh in Dan suggests that the two other expressions also refer to a form of Yahweh worship. אַשְׁמַת שֹׁמְרוֹן 'the guilt of Samaria' may refer to what Hosea calls 'the calf of Samaria' (Hos. 8.5 f.), so called because Yahweh is worshipped here too in the form of a bull image. In place of the proper oath formula Amos has contemptuously altered it to 'the guilt of Samaria', because the people have incurred guilt by worshipping Yahweh in this way (cf. Aaron according to Deut. 9.21 calling the golden calf 'your sin' חַטַּאתְכֶם). There is no evidence that Samaria is used by Amos for the whole Northern Kingdom, as some commentators have suggested. Why should the capital not also have had its bull image? This interpretation fits the context, and has the advantage that there is no need to alter the text. Others understand 'the guilt of Samaria' as a periphrasis for the Ashera pillar which Ahab had made, and which was still standing in the time of Jehoahaz (1 Kgs. 16.33; 2 Kgs. 13.6); some make the further assumption that the text originally ran אֲשֵׁרַת שֹׁמְרוֹן. This interpretation has the disadvantage that the reference is then to the worship not of Yahweh, but of the goddess Ashera (the female counterpart of Baal). The

---

[1] A parallel expression is the Arabic ġušiya 'alayhi 'he was covered over' = 'he fainted'.

same objection applies to a certain extent if we vocalize אֲשִׁמַת שׁ׳, so that the thought is of the goddess Ashima. She is known from 2 Kgs. 17.30, where an account is given of the different peoples whom the Assyrians allowed to settle in Samaria after the deportation of the Israelites, each of whom brought with them their own gods; so the people from Hamath made the goddess Ashima. This goddess is connected in one way or another with Ashim-Bethel, known from the Elephantine texts as a pair of deities connected with the worship of Yahweh (see A. Cowley, *Aramaic Papyri of the Fifth Century B.C.*, Oxford 1923, No. 22, line 124).[1] If Ashima had a place as the consort of Yahweh in Samaria, this would of course have evoked the disapproval of the prophet, but we would also certainly have expected a much more powerful attack against this cult. An attack on the Yahweh worship of Samaria on the other hand is in keeping with the other utterances of the prophet against the cultic centres (cf. 5.5). The last expression 'As the way of Beer-sheba lives', sounds strange in connection with the first two phrases. It has been explained by saying that the pilgrim route to the famous cultic centre of Beer-sheba (see on 5.5) was regarded as something fixed and unalterable, which was suitable for swearing by,[2] and it has been pointed out that the Semites do also treat as living some things which we regard as inanimate. But it cannot be denied that from the context we expect a reference to a divinity, or at least to the cult at Beer-sheba, not just to the way to the cultic centre. With this in view some suggest that we should understand דֶּרֶךְ in the sense of 'custom', i.e. cult. This view cannot be commended. Others give the more attractive solution that ר in דֶּרֶךְ is an error for דּ, so that the word can be read דֹּדְךָ 'your tutelary deity'. דֹּד means literally 'favourite' or 'near relative', but is also used as a name for God, cf. the personal name דֹּדָוָהוּ (2 Chron. 20.37), which should be read דּוֹדִיָהוּ 'Yahweh is the tutelary deity', and perhaps also the Mesha stone l. 12: אראל דודה 'the altar of its (i.e. the city's) tutelary deity' or '(the god) Daudo's altar' (*NSI*, p. 11, *KAI*,

---

[1] It is impossible to determine with certainty whether the first part of the name אשמבתאל is a god or a goddess at Elephantine. The form suggests the former, but a comparison with Anathbethel in No. 22, lines 123 ff. could indicate that this is the consort of the god Yahu. This view is further supported if Bethel in the compound name equals Yahu. The Phoenician god Eshmun can also be compared with the goddess Ashima (see *NSI*, pp. 30 ff., *KAI* No. 14).

[2] Cf. the Arab custom of swearing by the pilgrimage route to Mecca.

No. 181). This interpretation is supported by the LXX reading: ὁ θεός σου. Beer-sheba's tutelary deity cannot be other than Yahweh. A similar interpretation would be obtained by an alternative slight correction to הדרך 'your honour, Beer-sheba', i.e. Yahweh (ה could have fallen out after ך). The whole passage would then allude on the most probable interpretation to the worship of Yahweh at three different sanctuaries: (1) in Dan far to the north at the foot of Hermon, (2) in Samaria and (3) far to the south at Beer-sheba. The mention of these sanctuaries, at which it appears there were images of Yahweh, must not be treated as an isolated attack by Amos on the worship of images. The passage should be seen in the context of those passages in the book where he condemns the people for their cult because they thought that it was sufficient to worship Yahweh with sacrifices and feasts, and to take no notice of his ethical demands. The god that they worship and swear by is therefore not the true Yahweh, but a god that they have fashioned to their own desires)

The concluding words of v. 14 are parallel with the beginning of v. 13. But it is added that the fall is beyond remedy.

CHAPTER NINE

Vv. 1–4. The fifth vision: the temple is destroyed, and the whole people perishes

While the first two visions described how Yahweh at the prophet's intercession gave up his intention of destroying the people, and the next two declared that the disaster was inescapable, the fifth and last vision describes how it actually occurs. The occasion of the vision is presumably the autumn festival at Bethel, for which large crowds gather in the temple. The prophet is shocked by all that he sees, and proclaims Yahweh's destruction of the whole people, which is so to speak embodied in the participants in the feast. His description of the destruction suggests that he visualized it as a violent earthquake.

V. 1. The description of the vision is given in the first person. רָאִיתִי corresponds to כֹּה הִרְאַנִי in the other visions. Amos saw Yahweh standing at the side of the altar, in such a way that he towered up over it (cf. 1 Kgs. 13.1). The altar is probably, as has been suggested, the main altar in the temple at Bethel. If the MT is followed, Yahweh gives the order for the destruction of the columns, but it is not made clear whether the command is directed to the prophet or possibly to an angel who, it is implied, is there ready to carry out the command of Yahweh (cf. the seraphim in Isa. 6 and the angel in 2 Sam. 24.16). This lack of clarity is, however, to be preferred to the suggestion of several commentators, that we should read וַדֵּד in place of הַדֵּד and transfer וַיֹּאמֶר to before וּבְצַעַם, and in addition alter it to the first person in parallel to אֶהֱרֹג. כַּפְתּוֹר, literally 'knob', is here clearly a spherical decoration on the pillars (cf. Zeph. 2.14),[1] on which the rafters rest. We can translate 'heads of columns', or 'capitals' (taking it as a collective singular). The LXX reads ἱλαστήριον, but the MT is certainly correct here, since the word (although in a different sense) occurs again in v. 7 (on the catchword principle). The effect of the blow is so powerful that the whole temple shakes, and falls upon the heads of all who are in it, as when Samson broke the columns which held up the temple of Dagon (Judg. 16.29 f.). סַף (plur. סִפִּים) does not mean here 'the freestanding door-frame' (so F. Buhl, *Jesaja*, Copenhagen 1912, on Isa. 6.4), but 'the threshold of the door' (cf. Judg. 19.27), since the sense is that the shaking extends right down to the foundations of the temple. בְּצַעַם is an irregular imperative with suffix, for בְּצָעֵם from בָּצַע 'cut off'. The object of the command is the same as for הַדֵּד. The suffix in בְּצַעַם most probably refers to the collective כַּפְתּוֹר. On the other hand the suffix in כֻּלָּם refers to the participants in the festival in the temple. אַחֲרִיתָם 'what remains of them' may mean that Yahweh will slay those who survive the collapse of the temple, but may on the other hand be the equivalent of 'all of them to the last man' (cf. on 1.8 and 4.2). Vv. 2 ff. argue for the first interpretation. The last line of the verse emphasizes that the destruction will be complete.

V. 2. This and the following two verses elaborate how Yahweh will track down and overtake all who escape destruction in the first instance. חָתַר with בְּ: 'break through' (e.g. a wall, Ezek. 8.8) or, as here: 'break into'. The verb contains the idea that one must make an effort to break into the land of the dead, which is

---

[1] In Exod. 25.31 ff. it is a decoration on the arms of the golden candlesticks (RV knops, RSV capitals).

thought of as lying deep under the earth (cf. Isa. 14.15; Ezek. 32.18; Deut. 32.22; Job 26.5 f.). Elsewhere the land of the dead is thought of as a territory which is outside the reach of Yahweh (Ps. 88), and where no one gives heed to Yahweh (Ps. 6.6; 30.10; 115.17; Isa. 38.18). Here on the other hand Yahweh is Lord of the land of the dead, as in Ps. 139.8 ff. ('If I ascend to heaven, thou art there! If I make my bed in Sheol, thou art there! If I take the wings of the morning and dwell in the uttermost parts of the sea, even there thy hand shall lead me, and they right hand shall hold me.'). The land of the dead is perhaps originally the place of the family grave, but is in any case later the common gathering place for all the dead. The etymology of the word is unknown. The opposite of the land of the dead is heaven (cf. Isa. 7.11 in the versions of Aquila, Symmachus and Theodotion), and here Amos clearly does not stop to reflect that Yahweh is there already (cf. v. 6), so that he does not need to climb up there to fetch them. The passage simply wishes to say that there is no place in the whole universe where they can feel themselves secure against Yahweh.

V. 3 mentions two other places which are contrasted with one another, and where they might suppose they could hide themselves. Carmel is the well-known promontory which juts out into the Mediterranean (cf. on 1.2). It is well wooded, and on the cliffs towards the sea contains thousands of limestone caves with many narrow entrances, and with winding passages inside the mountain, so that there are hiding places enough here for a fugitive both above and below ground. In contrast to this high mountain overlooking the sea there is the sea bed (קַרְקַע הַיָּם) beneath it. Here too they will not be safe, because Yahweh will command the serpent to bite them. This does not refer to some kind of poisonous sea-serpent, which is supposed to live in the Mediterranean. It is a reminiscence of the old myth of creation, in which the story was told of Yahweh's fight with a monster, which he defeated. It is sometimes called רַהַב (Isa. 51.9; Ps. 89.11; Job 9.13; 26.12) sometimes לִוְיָתָן (Isa. 27.1; Ps. 74.14).[1] After the monster was de-

---

[1] We have evidence that the concept of this snake was taken over from the Canaanites, see from Ras Shamra 5(I *AB) I, 1 f.: 'When you have slain Lotan, the fleeing snake, destroyed the winding snake, the powerful one with seven heads . . .' The Canaanites in turn borrowed the concept from the Babylonians, who called the dragon Tiamat, תְּהוֹם of Gen. 1.2.

feated in the creation of the world, the myth probably also told
how it was banished for ever to the bottom of the sea. On the
relation between a command and its performance see on 6.11. The
second מִשָּׁם is probably an error for שָׁם (dittography), cf. v. 4.

V. 4. Nor will the Israelites be able to escape their fate, even if
they are carried away to a foreign land as prisoners before their
conquerors. For Yahweh's might no frontiers exist, just as he is
capable of knowing everything. הֲרַגְתָּם is perfect 3rd fem. with 3rd
plural suffix (Gr. § 59g). שִׂים עַיִן עַל 'turn one's eye to' can be used
in a good sense, 'look upon someone to protect them' (Jer. 24.6;
39.12), but here it is stressed that it has the opposite meaning, that
Yahweh will keep a watchful eye on them to punish them.

Vv. 5–6: A doxology of Yahweh's might in nature

These two verses are in form strongly reminiscent of 4.13 and
5.8 f. As has been said already these are regarded by many commentators as later insertions, and so is this passage too. But in all
three passages the description of Yahweh's might gives added
weight to the words of the prophet for his listeners, to let them
know that Yahweh has the power to carry out the threats which
the prophet utters. It is unjustifiable in principle to declare *a priori*
that Amos cannot have written these verses, because they inter-
rupt the preaching of judgement, which is in fact picked up again
after the doxology, or because they are divergent in style (see on
4.13).

V. 5. The whole sentence, which is introduced by וַאדֹנָי״, is
best translated: 'As truly as the Lord Yahweh of hosts, who
touches . . . his name is Yahweh.' All that comes in between is a
description of his might.[1] The verse describes the effects of an
earthquake. The introductory participle can be understood as a
description of Yahweh's might in general, but the consecutive
form וַתָּמוֹג suggests that the thought is of a single occasion in the
past. The same question arises again in v. 6b. וַתָּמוֹג is a pausal
form, from מוּג 'tremble'. The last line of v. 5 is almost identical
with 8.8.

V. 6 gives new proof of God's might by describing in poetic

---

[1] Grammatically it is also possible to translate 'but the Lord is Yahweh of hosts,
who . . .', or 'but the Lord Yahweh of hosts is he who touches . . .'.

language a similar image of the world to that which we find in Gen. 1: the firmament (called רָקִיעַ in Gen. 1.6; another word אֲגֻדָּה is used here, literally 'bound', 'bond') rests upon the earth, under which are the springs of the primeval deep. Above the firmament, in which the stars are placed, there are also bodies of water, which God can pour out over the earth by opening the sluice-gates of heaven (cf. Gen. 7.11). This passage goes beyond the picture in Genesis in saying that God has also built himself a dwelling place in heaven, that is, over the waters above the firmament (cf. Ps. 104.3). מַעֲלוֹתוֹ in the normal sense of the word would have to mean 'staircase', 'ascent' (plural of מַעֲלָה), but the מ may be a dittography; we could then read עֲלִיָּתוֹ 'his upper floor', that is, a room upon the flat roof of the house (see Judg. 3.20; 1 Kgs. 17.19, cf. ὑπερῷον Acts. 1.13). The view could perhaps be defended that we should take מעלות in the same sense as עֲלִיָּה. The second half-verse is identical with 5.8b. If the description is of God's might in general, the thought is of the rain. If on the other hand the verse is understood as referring to a single occasion (cf. the imperfect consecutive), the thought must be of the flood, or of a violent inundation.

V. 7: Israel is not worth more to Yahweh than are the other nations

This verse must be regarded as a refutation of an implied objection from the people, who boasted of Israel's election over against other nations, and asserted that election secured them against disaster. Against such an objection the prophet says to them outright that they must not think that they have an advantage at all, even over so despised a nation as the Cushites. כּוּשׁ is the name for the southern part of the Nile valley; the LXX usually translates it by Ethiopia, but it corresponds more closely to Nubia.[1] Its dark-skinned inhabitants were held in contempt by the Israelites. Gen. 10.6 ff. counts the Cushites as sons of Ham. The dark colour of the people's skins is alluded to in the often quoted saying in Jer. 13.23: 'If a Cushite (RSV Ethiopian) can change his skin, or a panther his stripes, then you too can do good.' כּוּשִׁי 'Cushite', plural כֻּשִׁיִּים. For בְּנֵי כֻשִׁיִּים one would expect

---

[1] It is around the land of Cush that according to Gen. 2.13 the river Gihon flows.

either כָּשִׁיִּים on its own or בְּנֵי כוּשׁ. Israel must not treat it as something unique that Yahweh has led them up from Egypt, because
he has also led up Israel's enemies the Philistines from Caphtor,
and the Aramaeans from Ķir. For the Philistines and Caphtor see
on 1.6 ff., for the Aramaeans and Ķir see on 1.5. This strong expression of Israel's status as equal with that of other nations contains a contradiction to 3.2, where the prophet gave Israel a
special status because of its election. But the point there was that
Israel had no entitlement to sin more than the others, because
Yahweh had chosen it; on the contrary this carried with it all the
greater obligations on the side of the people, and Yahweh would
not spare them for that reason. On this central point there is therefore agreement, even if the actual words of the two passages,
which are uttered passionately, do not agree in their view of the
election of the people. The tension between Yahweh's love for the
people and his judgement upon them is expressed in a similar
manner in 7.15 and 8.2, where Yahweh describes Israel as his own
people, although he sees that it is ready for punishment. Israel is
here used in its wider sense of the whole people, as appears from
the reference to the story of the Exodus.

Vv. 8–15: Description of the favourable future after the judgement, which only affects the wicked (vv. 8–10); the Davidic dynasty will be fully restored (vv. 11–12), the land will be abundantly fertile, and its inhabitants will no more be driven into exile (vv. 13–15)

The whole passage is regarded as secondary by the overwhelming majority of modern commentators. The arguments adduced
against its genuineness include firstly, that a perceptible alteration
in tone comes in with v. 8,[1] in that punishment is no longer for
all, as in vv. 1–4, but only for 'the sinful kingdom' (the Northern
Kingdom), and it is said that Yahweh will not completely exterminate the house of Jacob (i.e. both Israel and Judah); furthermore v. 9 speaks of a cleansing or purification, not of complete
destruction, and v. 10 says that sinners shall die by the sword,

---

[1] Compare Wellhausen's phrase (*Die Kleinen Propheten*, ed. 3, p. 96): 'Roses and
lavender instead of blood and iron'.

which serves as a corrective to the absolute extermination put before the people as their prospect in the preceding passage, especially in v. 1, where Yahweh says that he will destroy them all ('what remains of them') with the sword. Then this change in tone which has already been felt in v. 8 moves on to a promise from v. 11, so that the thought is now no longer of the sin of the people. A brilliant restoration for the house of David is predicted, accompanied by the recovery of lost dominion over the former subject nations round about; and in v. 13 a fertility is promised which stands in sharp contrast to the famine of 8.11; the devastated towns will be rebuilt (v. 14), and the people will dwell in them again without risk of being driven out (v. 15). Finally an indication has been found in the expression 'the fallen booth of David' in v. 11 of the fall of the Davidic dynasty in 586 B.C., so that the time of composition is exilic or post-exilic; and this is taken to be the implication of v. 15, which says that the people will be planted in their land, and not be cast off again. These points taken together are regarded as proof that the whole passage vv. 8–15 is a later addition to the book, intended to soften and correct the harsh threats which the Jews could not bear to read in the post-exilic period, when the people needed consolation and encouragement more than the preaching of affliction and disaster. Some of these objections, however, lose their strength when it is realized that these problems recur in other prophets. It is for instance not an isolated problem whether Amos in spite of everything could have had a faith in a brighter future for his people, though he has consistently and firmly expressed himself in the opposite sense. We are compelled to ask whether the prophets in general did not express themselves categorically in their preaching of judgement, because they were convinced that Yahweh must and would punish the people for their sins, if they did not show penitence and improvement. Yahweh's jealousy and holiness were incompatible with sin, and must therefore keep it at a distance. But at the same time the prophets also knew that Yahweh's grace and mercy were properties which he could not put aside without coming into conflict with his own innermost nature. The only way out in this conflict was to say that there were still some among the people who repented in time (when the prophets castigated their contemporaries and preached repentance, this must be because they thought that it was still not too late for repentance), or that the people would undergo a purification, so that all that was unclean would be excluded, after which Yahweh would restore what remained, and give it a future of good fortune, in accordance with the covenant he had made with the people in the earliest times. The question arises in this form for Hosea, Isaiah and Micah, who all lived at roughly the same time as Amos, and for Jeremiah about a hundred years later. Hosea castigates the people and predicts their fall, but yet believes in the people's restoration after a period of cleansing (2.14–23; 3; 14). Isaiah speaks with equal harshness to his countrymen in Judah, but yet puts his trust in the remnant which will repent, and expects that a descendant of David will fulfil the prophecies which were attached to the Davidic dynasty (chapters 9 and 11). Micah too speaks in quite as strong terms as Amos of the sin of the people, and actually predicts the destruction of Jerusalem and of the temple (3.12), but nonetheless believed in a future of good fortune (chapters 4–5); and the same is true of Jeremiah, in whose book prophecies of judgement and promises are found side by side. It would therefore not be without analogy if Amos had in spite of all expected that Yahweh would be able to fulfil his promises at some time in the future, when he had punished the people.

The pattern of misfortune linked with good fortune has also been demonstrated in Egyptian oracles, e.g. in the prophecy of Neferrohu from *c.* 2000 B.C.[1] Here the transition from prophecy of judgement to promise is quite as abrupt as in Amos. This has persuaded several commentators to change their minds and allow the possible authenticity of the promises in the prophets of the Old Testament. More generally, the change from misfortune to good fortune is found in Oriental dramas, in which both parts belong together to create the correct balance in life. Men of antiquity could therefore contain these contradictions in themselves. In the most recent scholarly work the view has been taken that the prophets took over this pattern from the cult. The question needs a full treatment which it is not possible to give it here. It must, however, be declared firmly that for the prophets the promises must have been ethically based in

---

[1] A. H. Gardiner, 'New Literary Works from Ancient Egypt', *Journal of Egyptian Archaeology* I (1914), pp. 101–6.

9*

the nature of Yahweh; only in this way can they be reconciled with the preaching of judgement.

As a Judean, Amos like Isaiah and Micah had grown up with the hopes that were placed in the line of David, and similarly regarded the division of the kingdoms as a breach which had never been healed (cf. Isa. 7.17). He may well therefore have regarded the Davidic dynasty as fallen in relation to David's own time, in which Israel was one kingdom, and furthermore had power over all its neighbours, and speak of 'building up the breach in it'. As for exile, it was a punishment with which he had threatened the people; it was indeed one of the main points in Amaziah's complaint about him to the king (7.11). Amos therefore was looking for the deportation of the people, and it is only a continuation of a leading idea in his preaching if he says that after enduring the punishment they will no more be cast off. We cannot therefore conclude from this expression that the prophet lives in or after the exile. It only remains to consider whether the exile will also affect Judah. If 2.4–5 are by Amos (see above), he also looked for a punishment of Judah (cf. 6.1). It is therefore not impossible that he thought that its population would share the fate of the people of the Northern Kingdom, and be purified by deportation. But it is by no means certain. Judah could also have been punished in a milder way, e.g. by being ravaged by hostile armies. We are not in a position to solve this problem, because his utterances about Judah are just too brief. If the whole of the conclusion is by Amos, he hoped that Judah after enduring the punishment of the nation would take over the leadership as in the time of David in a united Israelite kingdom, having dominion over the surrounding nations. We must recognize that this is uncertain; nor are we in a position to decide whether Amos reached this view during his stay in the Northern Kingdom or only after his expulsion.

V. 8. Since Yahweh speaks in v. 8b, we could have expected עֵינַי without אדני יהוה. The change of person is not impossible, but we must also consider the possibility that the text originally had עיני, which was meant as a dual with suffix, but that the form was understood as a construct, and אדני יהוה inserted for this reason. In a phrase which reminds us of v. 4b, it is said that the eyes of Yahweh are directed against the sinful kingdom to destroy it; the thought here can only be of the Northern Kingdom. V. 8c on the

other hand provides a limitation (אֶפֶס כִּי 'only that' i.e. 'nevertheless') by saying that Yahweh will not utterly[1] destroy 'the
house of Jacob'. This expression can, like 'the house of Israel' in
v. 9, mean the Northern Kingdom (see 5.1, 4; 6.14; 7.10, cf. also
7.2, 5; 8.7). What follows should be to the effect that in spite of
everything there were good elements in Israel, which were to survive deportation. Since, however, the kingdom of Judah is
brought into the prophecy from v. 11, we cannot avoid the conclusion that 'the house of Jacob' and 'the house of Israel' in vv. 8
and 9 are descriptions for all Israel (cf. 6.1). The good elements,
which will survive the process of purification, are perhaps to be
found especially in the south.

V. 9. The people will be shaken among (בְּ—not 'together
with') the other nations, as corn is shaken round in a sieve when
it is to be winnowed. יִנּוֹעַ is an impersonal passive, 'it is shaken'.
The passage speaks of a scattering among all the nations in contrast to 6.14, which only speaks of one nation (the Assyrians).
But this cannot be said to be a compelling reason for denying the
verse to Amos, since the punishment all through the book is represented in widely differing forms, earthquake, famine, war
with destruction of cities and their inhabitants, deportation, etc.
In illumination of this passage we can refer to the way the win-
nowing of corn was done until recently in Syria. כְּבָרָה 'sieve' may
refer to the coarse sieve (Arabic *kirbāl*), through which the corn
is first passed after the threshing. This sieves out the stones, clods
of earth, etc., while the corn passes through. צְרוֹר can in that case
be taken in the sense of 'stone' (2 Sam. 17.13). This type of sieve
is also used by bricklayers, when they pass the fine sand which
they use for mortar through a sieve to separate out the larger
stones. Others, however, think here of the fine sieve (Arabic
ġirbāl), which is used after the first sieving. This fine sieve lets the
chaff and dust go through, while the grains are left behind. However, צְרוֹר would have to mean 'corn', if this interpretation is to
be maintained. But there is no attestation for this meaning of the
word. We must therefore maintain the former meaning of כְּבָרָה,
and the thought is that the wicked people are sifted out and do
not survive exile. On the second interpretation the passage would

---

[1] This is definitely how the expression should be translated. It would also be possible to
translate, 'I will not at all destroy the house of Jacob'. But the context supports the first
translation.

mean that none of the good people would be lost in exile. The first view fits best the context, which speaks of the destruction of sinners.

V. 10 emphasizes that destruction is the fate of sinners. These are more precisely characterized in the second half of the verse as arrogant men, who look forward to peace and good fortune. Since תַּגִּישׁ cannot so well be taken as an intransitive, the subject must be Yahweh: 'You will not let evil overtake us'. It is better to vocalize it as a qal, and to take הָרָעָה as the subject: 'evil will not reach us', cf. for this the LXX and the Syriac translation. Correspondingly it is better to read the piel תְּקַדֵּם in place of the hiphil (the hiphil of קדם occurs otherwise only in Job 41.3, where the text is not certain). The preposition בַּעַד nearly always has the meaning 'apart from', 'barring'; most commentators therefore in place of בַּעֲדֵינוּ read עָדֵינוּ 'to us'. For the words of arrogant men cf. also Isa. 5.19 and Jer. 23.17.

V. 11. בַּיּוֹם הַהוּא 'on that day' points to the day when Yahweh will again have mercy on the people, after they have endured their punishment. In other contexts Amos uses 'that day' of the day of judgement (8.3, 9 and 13). סֻכָּה means a hut made of branches, for instance of the sort that men dwelt in during the feast of booths. It is here meant to symbolize that the dynasty or kingdom of David (בֵּית דָּוִיד, cf. 2 Sam. 7.5, 11) is now not a house, but a simple hut. The hut is further described as נֹפֶלֶת. The participle could be translated 'falling', i.e. ready to fall down, but since there is a reference to raising it, it must here mean 'fallen'. For what the event is to which reference is being made, see the introductory remarks to this section. In the rest of the verse expressions are used which do not fit a hut made of branches, but a damaged house, which is to be built up again and improved, so that it becomes as it originally was. The suffixes in פִּרְצֵיהֶן and הֲרִסֹתָיו are in disorder; it is best to read them both as feminine singulars, referring back to the word סֻכָּה. פֶּרֶץ 'crack', 'hole' or 'breach in a wall' (see 4.3). *הֲרִיסָה (from הרס) 'that is pulled down' (only here in the Old Testament, but also in Sirach 49.13). עוֹלָם need not be the earliest times, but can also be the distant past. In relation to Amos' time the time of David could well be described as עוֹלָם.

V. 12. The subject of יִירְשׁוּ does not appear immediately from the text; one may think of the rulers of the Davidic dynasty, or

perhaps just of the Israelites in general. A restoration is pro-
phesied of Israel's might as it was in the time of David, when the
Edomites, the Philistines, the Aramaeans, the Moabites and the
Ammonites were subordinate to it. After the death of David
Israel's suzerainty declined fast, and Israel itself was divided
after the death of Solomon. 'The remnant of Edom' has been
taken as evidence of a later date, when things went harshly for
Edom (cf. Mal. 1.3, 4), but there is no difficulty in thinking that
Amos has used this expression on the grounds of Israel's hostility
to Edom, to deride it by prophesying that it too would meet with
a great disaster. 'The remnant of Edom' could also mean 'Edom
down to its last fragment' (cf. 'the remnant of the Philistines', 1.8
and 4.2). LXX (Codex B) reads ὅπως ἐκζητήσωσιν οἱ κατά-
λοιποι τῶν ἀνθρώπων, i.e. it reads יִדְרְשׁוּ in place of יִירְשׁוּ and
אָדָם in place of אֱדוֹם, and omits אֶת־ before שְׁאֵרִית. Acts 15.17,
which quotes this passage, adds the object τὸν κύριον, which is
also found in Codex A in the LXX. MT is of course the original
text. To 'name one's name over something' means to acknowl-
edge it as one's property (see 2 Sam. 12.28; Isa. 63.19; Jer. 7.10;
Dan. 9.18 f., cf. already in the Amarna letters 'to lay one's name
on a land' meaning 'to take it in possession').[1] The nations listed
had been the property of Yahweh when David made them subject
to Israel. The oracle concludes with the regular phrase נְאֻם יהוה,
to which is added an assurance that he will really do what has
been said in the preceding passage.

V. 13. The description of the future fertility of the land is
introduced by a phrase which in itself is neutral, 'Behold, the days
are coming'. In 4.2 and 8.11 the context told us that they would
be bad days, but here they will be days of good fortune (cf. Jer.
16.14 f.). Fertility will be so great that the work of ploughing and
the work of reaping will catch up with one another, and similarly
the pressing of grapes and the sowing. More precisely it must mean
that the crops grow so fast that the ploughman is hardly finished
breaking up the earth for sowing before the corn is already ripe for
harvest, nor is it possible to get the treading of the grapes finished
before it is time to sow. Barley and wheat harvest take place in
April and May, the vine-gathering not till September. Ploughing

---

[1] See H. Zimmern, 'Palästina um das Jahr 1400 vor Chr. nach neuen Quellen', *Zeitschrift des Deutschen Palästina-Vereins*, 13 (1890), p. 140, and J. A. Knudtzon, *Die el-
Amarna Tafeln*, Leipzig 1915, p. 867 (Letter 287, ll. 60 ff.).

comes in the month of October, when the rain begins to fall
again, so that the ground which has been dry and hard as stone
becomes workable again. After this sowing can take place in
November.[1] V.13a therefore describes the speed of growth of the
crops, v. 13b the overwhelming quantity of the crops. The verb
נגש in the niphal with בְּ is best translated as 'overtake' (cf. KB).

Lev. 26.5 contains a similar promise to that which we have
here. We would expect הַחֹרֵשׁ (with the article), parallel to the following 'reaper'. The treading of the grapes is done by a man
treading (דְּרַךְ) the grapes in a press (גַּת), from which the juice
flows down into a bowl (יֶקֶב) (see *BRL*, col. 538, *IDB* s.v.
Wine, vol. 4, pp. 849 ff.). מָשַׁךְ 'draw', 'pull': 'to draw seed' refers
either to the arm movement of the sower when he sows, or perhaps better to the seed being sown in long rows. V. 13b describes
the enormous quantity of wine which the vine slopes will yield.
The expressions remind us in their content of the well-known
phrase 'a land flowing with milk and honey' (Exod. 3.17, 13.5
and elsewhere), and is almost word for word identical with Joel
4.18; where, however, in contrast to the passage in Amos milk is
also mentioned. We do not necessarily have reciprocal influence
between the two prophetic passages, since the expressions used
are stock phrases. עָסִיס (literally 'that which is crushed' or
'pressed', from עסס) is a new only lightly fermented wine.[2] מוג in
the hithpolel 'be melted', 'be softened' (cf. the polel 'make
something firm stagger or melt', e.g. of the rain, which softens
the earth, Ps. 65.11). The idea is certainly that the juice will over-
flow the vats in the vinepressing, and flow down the slopes of the
hills, so that they are softened. A pre-exilic date for the passage
can be supported by the fact that descriptions of the fertility of
the land already occur in the Ras Shamra texts in connection with
the good fortune that comes when Baal takes over the royal
power at the beginning of the rainy season. It is said in this connection 'the heavens let it rain with fatness, and the valleys flow
with honey' (1 AB III, 6 ff.). This is an argument for claiming that
the prophetic descriptions of the fertility of the land are taken over
from Canaanite patterns.

V. 14. In the phrase שׁוּב שְׁבוּת some understand the word שְׁבוּת

---

[1] On this see G. Dalman, *Arbeit und Sitte in Palästina*, II, Gütersloh 1932, pp. 177, 198,
and IV, Gütersloh 1935, pp. 368 f.
[2] The unfermented grape-juice is called תִּירֹשׁ.

as 'captivity': it is better, however, to derive the word from שׁוּב,
so that the whole expression means 'to turn a turning', i.e. 'restore'. If the word comes from שׁוּב, one would have expected a
full qameṣ in the first syllable. The weak vowel can be explained
by assimilation to the word שְׁבִית 'captivity', which the Massoretes
connected it with. V. 14b and c are in contrast to 4.9, and especially
to 5.11. A similar promise is found in Isa. 65.21. 'Israel' is here
again used of the whole nation (cf. on 2.6).

V. 15. In the introductory remarks to vv. 8–15 arguments
have been given to support the view that the promise of the
people's future undisturbed habitation of the land does not
necessarily presuppose the exile as an event that has already taken
place, and an attempt has been made in general to meet objections
to the authenticity of the passage. The possibility has been maintained that Amos was in line with the other pre-exilic prophets in
his views of a brighter future after the punishment which he undoubtedly expected must be imminent for the people. But it must
be granted that in total there are so many uncertainties in the
understanding of individual elements in these verses, that it
would not be correct to hold firmly to the view that the whole of
the conclusion must go back to Amos in the form in which it is
transmitted here. One cannot neglect the possibility that the conclusion may have been reworked and now bears the stamp of the
subsequent fate of the people.

The book concludes by emphasizing that the promise is
uttered by 'Yahweh your God', so that the people are assured
that Yahweh will now be again the protector of the people, and
not as previously (4.2) come in judgement.

BIBLIOGRAPHY

COMMENTARIES:

Bewer, J. A., *The Book of the Twelve Prophets*, Harper's Annotated Bible, vol. 2, New York 1949

Cripps, R. S., *A Critical and Exegetical Commentary on the Book of Amos*, London 1929, ed. 2, 1955

Driver, S. R., *The Books of Joel and Amos*, Cambridge Bible for Schools and Colleges, ed. 2, rev. by H. C. O. Lanchester, Cambridge 1915

Edghill, E. A., *The Book of Amos*, Westminster Commentaries, London 1914, ed. 2, 1926

Ewald, H., *Die Propheten des Alten Bundes*, Göttingen 1840, ed. 2, 1867, ET by J. F. Smith, *Commentary on the Prophets of the Old Testament*, vol. 1, London 1875

Gressmann, H., *Die Älteste Geschichtsschreibung und Prophetie Israels*, Die Schriften des Alten Testaments, 2. Abt., 1. Band, Göttingen 1921

Guthe, H., in *Die Heilige Schrift des Alten Testaments*, ed. E. Kautsch, ed. 4, ed. A. Bertholet, Tübingen 1923

Harper, W. R., *A Critical and Exegetical Commentary on Amos and Hosea*, International Critical Commentary, Edinburgh 1905

Hoonacker, A. van, *Les Douze Petits Prophètes*, Études Bibliques, Paris 1908

Koehler, L., *Amos*, Zürich 1917

Marti, K., *Das Dodekapropheton*, Kurzer Hand-Commentar zum Alten Testament, XIII, Tübingen 1904

Michelet, S., *Amos oversat og fortolket*, Christiania 1893

Mowinckel, S., *Det Gamle Testamente* oversatt av Michelet, Mowinckel og Messel, vol. 3, Oslo 1944

Nowack, W., *Die Kleinen Propheten*, Handkommentar zum Alten Testament, Göttingen 1897, ed. 3, 1922

Robinson, T. H. (with F. Horst), *Die Zwölf Kleinen Propheten*, Handbuch zum Alten Testament, Tübingen 1938, ed. 2, 1954, ed. 3, 1964

Schmidt, H. *Der Prophet Amos. 6 Vorlesungen*, Tübingen 1917

Sellin, E., *Das Zwölfprophetenbuch*, Kommentar zum Alten Testament 12, Leipzig, ed. 1, 1922, ed. 2–3, 1929

Smith, G. A., *The Book of the Twelve Prophets*, The Expositor's Bible, London 1896, ed. 2, 1928

Weiser, A., *Das Buch der Zwölf Kleinen Propheten*, Das Alte Testament Deutsch, Göttingen 1949, ed. 2, 1956, ed. 3–4, 1959

Wellhausen, J., *Die Kleinen Propheten*, ed. 3, Berlin 1898 (reprinted 1963)

Wolff, H. W., *Dodekapropheton—Amos*, Biblischer Kommentar 14, fasc. 6–, Neukirchen–Vluyn 1967–

OTHER ARTICLES AND BOOKS ABOUT AMOS

Bentzen, A. 'The Ritual Background of Amos 1.2–2.16', *OTS* 8 (Leiden 1950), pp. 85–99

Budde, K., 'Zu Text und Auslegung des Buches Amos', *Journal of Biblical Literature* 43 (1924), pp. 46–131, 44 (1925), pp. 63–122

Carlson, A., 'Profeten Amos och Davidsriket', *RoB* 8 (1949), pp. 57–78

Cramer, K., *Amos, Versuch einer Theologischen Interpretation*, Beiträge zur Wissenschaft vom Alten und Neuen Testament 51, Stuttgart 1930

Danell, G. A., 'Var Amos verkligen en nabi?', *SEÅ* 16 (1952), pp. 7–20

Duhm, B., 'Anmerkungen zu den Zwölf Propheten. I. Buch Amos', *ZAW* 31 (1911), pp. 1–18

Dykema, F., 'Le Fond des Prophéties d'Amos', *OTS* 2 (Leiden 1943), pp. 18–34

Engnell, I., 'Profetismens ursprung och uppkomst', *RoB* 8 (1949), pp. 1–18

Farr, G., 'The Language of Amos, Popular or Cultic?', *VT* 16 (1966), pp. 312–24

Gese, H., 'Kleine Beiträge zum Verständnis des Amosbuches', *VT* 12 (1962), pp. 417–38

Gordis, R., 'The Composition and Structure of Amos', *Harvard Theological Review* 33 (1940), pp. 239–51

Gunneweg, A. H. J., 'Erwägungen zu Amos 7.14', *Zeitschrift für Theologie und Kirche* 57 (1960), pp. 1–16

Halévy, J. 'Recherches Bibliques. Le Livre d'Amos', *Revue Sémitique* 11 (1903), pp. 1–31, 97–121, 193–209, 289–300; 12 (1904) pp. 1–18

Hesse, F., 'Amos 5.4–6.14 f.', *ZAW* 68 (1956), pp. 1–17

Hyatt, J. P., 'The Translation and Meaning of Amos 5.23–24', *ZAW* 68 (1956), pp. 17–24

Jozaki, S., 'The Secondary Passages of the Book of Amos', *Kwansei Gakuin University Annual Studies* 4 (1956), pp. 25–100

Kapelrud, A. S., *Central Ideas in Amos* (Skrifter utgitt av Det Norske Videnskaps-Akademi i Oslo II. Hist.-Filos. Klasse 1956 No. 4), Oslo 1956 (reprinted 1961)

—— 'New Ideas in Amos', *Volume du Congrès Génève 1965*, SVT 15 (1966), pp. 193–206

Maag, V., *Text, Wortschatz und Begriffswelt des Buches Amos*, Leiden 1951

Morgenstern, J., *Amos Studies*, Cincinnati 1941

Neher, A., *Amos, contribution à l'étude du prophétisme*, Paris 1950

Neubauer, K. W., 'Erwägungen zu Amos 5.4–15', *ZAW* 78 (1966), pp. 292–316

Reventlow, H. Graf, *Das Amt des Propheten bei Amos*, FRLANT 80, Göttingen 1962

Rowley, H. H., 'Was Amos a Nabi?', *Festschrift Otto Eissfeldt*, Halle 1947, pp. 191–8

Schmidt, W., 'Die deuteronomische Redaktion des Amosbuches', *ZAW* 77 (1965), pp. 168–93

Seierstad, J. P., *Die Offenbarungserlebnisse der Propheten Amos, Jesaja und Jeremia*, Oslo 1946

Smend, R., 'Das Nein des Amos', *Evangelische Theologie* 23 (1963), pp. 404–23

Speier, S., 'Bemerkungen zu Amos', *VT* 3 (1953), pp. 305–10

Stoebe, H. J., 'Der Prophet Amos und sein Bürgerlicher Beruf', *Wort und Dienst* (Jahrbuch der Theologischen Schule Bethel), NF 5 (1957), pp. 160–81

Watts, J. D. W., 'An Old Hymn Preserved in the Book of Amos', *JNES* 15 (1956), pp. 33–9

—— *Vision and Prophecy in Amos*, Leiden 1958

Weiser, A., *Die Prophetie des Amos*, Beihefte zur Zeitschrift für die Alttestamentliche Wissenschaft 53, Giessen 1929

Wolff, H. W. *Amos' geistige Heimat*, Wissenschaftliche Monographien zum Alten und Neuen Testament 18, Neukirchen–Vluyn 1964

Würthwein, E., 'Amos-Studien', *ZAW* 62 (1950), pp. 10–52

—— 'Amos 5.21–27', *Theologische Literaturzeitung* 72 (1947), cols. 143–52

—— 'Kultpolemik oder Kultbescheid?', *Tradition und Situation*, Festschrift Artur Weiser, Göttingen 1963, pp. 115–31

Reference may also be made to the larger presentations of the history of Israel, to Introductions to the Old Testament and to histories of the religion of the Old Testament, and also to specialized works on prophecy, especially:

Buttenwieser, M., *The Prophets of Israel from the Eighth to the Fifth Century*, New York 1914

Duhm, B., *Israels Propheten*, ed. 2, Göttingen 1922

Gunkel, H., *Die Propheten*, Göttingen 1917

Hölscher, G., *Die Profeten. Untersuchungen zur Religionsgeschichte Israels*, Leipzig 1914

Lindblom, J., *Prophecy in Ancient Israel*, Oxford 1962

Smith, W. R., *The Prophets of Israel*, ed. 2, London 1895

Erling Hammershaimb is Professor
of Semitic Studies, University of
Aarhus, Denmark. John Sturdy is Dean
of Gonville and Caius College,
Cambridge.